It Was
Better
in the
Backseat

It Was
Better
in the
Backseat

HOW TO RECHARGE
YOUR SEX LIFE

Sherry Lehman, M.A.
and
Micki Brook

BOB ADAMS, INC.
Holbrook, Massachusetts

Published by Bob Adams, Inc.
260 Center Street, Holbrook, MA 02343

ISBN: 1-55850-359-5

Printed in the United States of America.

J   I   H   G   F   E   D   C   B   A

Library of Congress Cataloging-in-Publication Data
Lehman, Sherry.
    It was better in the backseat / Sherry Lehman, Micki Brook.
        p.   cm.
    Includes bibliographical references and index.
    ISBN 1-55850-359-5
    1. Sex instruction for women. 2. Women–Sexual behavior. 3. Sexual excitement. 4. Sex in marriage. I. Brook, Micki. II. Title.
    HQ46.L38   1994
    306.7'07–dc20
                                                                94-8715
                                                                CIP

This publication is designed to provide accurate and authoritative information with regard to the subject matter covered. It is sold with the understanding that the publisher is not engaged in rendering legal, accounting, or other professional advice. If legal advice or other expert assistance is required, the services of a competent professional person should be sought.
— From a *Declaration of Principles* jointly adopted by a Committee of the American Bar Association and a Committee of Publishers and Associations

This book is available at quantity discounts for bulk purchases.
For information, call 1-800-872-5627.

Cover photo ©1993 GlamourShots®
Cover design by Joyce C. Weston

To my mother and father, Esther and Marvin Friedman,
who have loved me, been there for me, and believed in me.
–S. L.

To my husband, Marvin G. Brook, M.D., for his professional
expertise as well as his continuous emotional support.
– M. B.

Contents

Acknowledgments

We will be forever indebted to our agent, Laurie Harper, who believed in our book and encouraged us beyond all expectation. Special thanks go to our excellent editor at Bob Adams, Inc., Laura Morin, for her constant support and insightful suggestions; to our publicist at Bob Adams, Donna Greer, who has worked zealously for exceptional publicity; and to the entire staff for their untold hours of diligence.

Kenneth Goodman, M.D., deserves a very special thanks for his computer expertise. Without his technical knowledge we would have been lost. We thank our good friend and fellow author Peggy Vaughan for her significant contributions, advice, and support.

We are eternally grateful to Drs. Kathleen R. and Nozar Alaolmolki and gynecologist Ivy Lee for their counsel, input, and guidance, and to the endless list of medical and psychology experts who suggested resources, explored issues, and discussed chapters.

— S. L. & M.B.

My love and gratefulness go to my family, especially to my sons, Jonathan and Michael, and to my sisters, Shelly Friedman, Marsha Friedman, and Bonnie Sanchez. Their tireless support and encouragement when I needed it the most carried me though some long days and nights. Thanks from the bottom of my heart to my dear friend and housekeeper, Alma, and to all my dear friends who have stood by me throughout the years, believed in me no matter what, and been there for the great times and the tough times. And I certainly want to acknowledge all of my patients who have taught me so much about love, sex, and life. Their stories are woven throughout the pages of this book; they have given me so much.

—S. L.

This book could not have been written without the wisdom and support of so many. I want to thank my children, Jeff and Maryann Fingerhut, Gary and Nancy Fingerhut, Bradley, and Ellen and Roger Brook, for endless hours of discussion and enlightening input. I am grateful for the patience of my friends during the writing of this book and for a long list of people who shared their personal experiences so candidly in the true stories that are reflected in its pages. And, last but not least, it is with unending gratitude I thank my mother, Anne Epstein, who has been my role model for successful living and loving.

—M. B.

Introduction

The phrase "It was better in the backseat" brings a smile to most people's faces. We remember the excitement and enthusiasm of necking with the boy next door. No matter how tentative our sexual prowess was back then, it is with great fondness most of us remember those early sexual experiences. Who of us would not like to bring back the sexual exuberance of those early years? Yet, today we seem more interested in the final destination than the actual journey. Our sex lives are apathetic. Our partners seem to apply the "dip stick" test to determine when we are "ready." The dip stick test is hardly going to increase a woman's sexual response; in many of us it just causes resentment. Very often the end or climax seems all our partners are concerned about. What about the delight and maddening anticipation along the way? How can a woman tell her mate what really turns her on without sounding like his teacher or his mother?

Women are often unsure how to tell men in a sensitive, effective way about their feelings about sex. They are afraid of how their partners will respond . . . with anger, rejection, or withdrawal. Many men are not receptive to hearing *anything* about this intimate subject, and women have not, as yet, found the way to make them more responsive. This book gives both advice and solutions to a woman's concerns about sex. It will help women become more comfortable with their emotions and sexual feelings, understand what those feelings are, and learn how and when to express them. This book shows a woman how to speak to her man, to help him understand what she wants and needs sexually.

Despite the humorous title, this book deals seriously with what all partners need to know about how and when to talk to a mate so that individual needs will be understood and responded to. Mates can learn to feel more comfortable expressing these needs and wants to a partner. Courage and confidence can become yours with the help of this book, your own personal sex therapist.

You may recognize many of your personal situations in the true cases told by my patients over twenty years. Their stories are altered only for the purpose of maintaining privacy. You will be able to apply many of the solutions offered in these pages to recapture the love life for which you yearn.

Each of us wishes to regain the excitement, the sense of urgency, and most of all, the intensity with which we stroked, groped, touched, and explored when we first fell in love. Few of us were sexual experts back then. Individual fantasies about the charms and desirability of our partners and the idea that we were sexually desired carried the day (or night). Being wanted and welcomed by one very special person is still the key to exciting, satisfying sex. The importance of making a partner *feel* needed and welcome is something couples hear about all the time. But how do partners evoke those intimate feelings? This book will help you recognize what is keeping you from telling your mate exactly what the problems are. Rest assured that you are not alone. Most couples experience problems at one time or another during a relationship. Almost all partners need help to determine what to say and when to say it in a caring yet effective way. This is really the heart of successful relationships.

Although many partners yearn to experience powerfully passionate feelings with their mates, few believe the initial experiences of sex can ever be recaptured. Couples hear repeatedly that confronting problems is a difficult and painful process that most mates try to avoid. No one wishes to court failure. This book helps reaffirm that it is possible for each person to build a sexual romantic life. Each partner does possess the ability to cooperate and negotiate with a mate in a loving and caring manner. Old habits can be unlearned. Almost all mates can learn to accept one's self and one's partner. Successful loving is a challenge, but it is a challenge that is worthwhile.

CHAPTER 1

I'll Show You Mine if You Show Me Yours

Although there are many similarities between men and women, there are also definite differences. Often the differences that attract men and women to each other initially are the very things that cause problems later in the relationship. A woman may be attracted to a strong and silent type both in and out of bed. Years later, his silence may irritate her and leave her feeling lonely.

Other women may be mystified by their mates' sexual reactions. What she may feel is sexually logical and explicit often goes unnoticed and ignored by her partner. What seems perfectly reasonable to her may seem completely irrational to him. Many are bewildered about why what began as an exciting sex life now seems fraught with anxiety and boredom.

A woman has just returned from a lovely evening with her special man. Dinner was delicious and the movie was erotic. She is excited and anticipates an exciting adventure in bed. He, too, is aroused. He rubs her in places that make her feel as though he is kneading bread on her body. He tells her how sexy Kathleen Turner was in the movie, not how sexy she is. She feels he is exploring her body by rote. His urgency rushes him to climax. She is wondering where all the romantic feelings she brought to bed have gone.

This situation is certainly not unique. So many women find themselves in this same predicament. Yet many women do not know how to change a mate's disappointing responses into a riveting sexual encounter. A woman feels she is giving off all the right signals.

What can she do when his reaction is so different from what she hopes for?

The story of Sybil and Jim, a couple very much in love, is a typical example of a sex life gone awry. They had been married for three years when Sybil first sought therapy.

> "There are times of the month I find I'm just not in the mood for sex at all. I feel 'shut down' sexually. I would rather be looking through a cookbook. Everything annoys me. The way he slurps his soup, crackles the paper as he turns the pages, yawns with his mouth uncovered . . . I want to strangle him."

The 'thirtysomething', tall, lanky blond sitting in my office was close to erupting with frustration. Sybil had requested an immediate appointment, saying her marriage was at stake. She came into the office with hair flying and spaghetti sauce decorating her shirt and jeans. It was obvious that Sybil felt she was at a breaking point.

> "Just this very morning, while I was trying to butter Timmy's toast and make Jim some instant coffee, what does Jim do? He pats me on the rear end and suggests we put Timmy in front of the television and go back to bed for a 'quickie'. He could see that I was busy and not in the mood, or is he blind? Can you believe it?"

Her frustration *was* believable. How many times had tearful wives described similar situations?

> "Jim just can't understand why one day I'm in the mood the minute he walks through the door, and the next day I'm like a dead salmon when he tries to approach me. There are times I behave like two different people. A touch I found wonderfully exciting yesterday feels like someone scratching chalk on a blackboard the next day. I really don't know what to say to him. I don't understand it myself. It really has nothing to do with him. It's *me* and I know it, but when he presses me to tell him what is wrong, I can't say that I'm just not in the mood at all. What's wrong with me?"

What Sybil is experiencing is not at all unusual. A woman's sexual mood tends to fluctuate with her menstrual cycle. As the estrogen level changes, many women experience an increase or decrease in sex drive. For instance, Sybil reported feeling more sexual during ovulation and for a few days before her period and did not feel sexual at all after her period.

Not realizing this, Jim did not pick up on the signals that Sybil was not in the mood. That she was wearing her old flannel nightgown and schleppy robe with food stains all over it was not obvious enough. When she told Jim to go to work instead of back to the bedroom, he felt Sybil was rejecting him. Sybil needs to tell Jim that it was not *him*. Her refusal to make love was because she was feeling tense and unattractive, and that made her react to the crunch of his cereal and the rattle of his paper. It was because, clean-shaven and fresh, dressed in his suit and tie for the office, he looked better than she did. She was feeling fat, ugly, and bloated in her messy robe.

It is not realistic to assume that a man can tell when his mate is feeling sexy and when she is not. To him, she might look beautiful all the time. So when he makes advances and she ends up telling him to go to work instead of to bed, it is not surprising that he leaves, slamming the door behind him. Then she is left feeling angry because he acts as though she can be turned on and off, like the flick of a switch.

What can Sybil do to keep this sort of scene from happening again and again? First of all, if she is not already doing so, she needs to keep track of her menstrual cycle. She should explain to Jim how and when her hormonal level affects her sex drive. Alternatively, Sybil could help Jim chart her cycle. That way, he will be more aware of her sexual highs and lows.

Sybil can tell Jim that it is not his fault; that he may need to take more time with her when she's in low gear. She can even use numbers to let him know where she is on the sexual mood scale. "One" could mean, "Dynamite won't work tonight!" and "ten" could mean, "Look at me and I'm yours!"

For instance, when Jim made his first move, Sybil could have told him that she felt like a "one" ("Dynamite won't work"), but with his patience and understanding, maybe by tonight she would feel like a "six" or maybe even a "seven." This tells him it is not *his* fault. He is adorable. *She* loves him and regrets how *she* feels now, but she is looking forward to feeling passionate with him later.

Women need to reassure their partners that they are loved and desired. It is a good idea to promise a future sex date, maybe tomorrow, or even tonight. This should not be left open ended. A woman should tell her mate when there will be time to cuddle and how much his understanding is needed. His sensitivity to her problem can help her climb from a "one" to an "eight." It is best for her to say all of this right then and there so he does not feel upset and rejected.

It is even better if a woman can convey her feelings before a sexual overture is made. It is difficult, if not impossible, for couples to check their sexual moods every moment of the day. One way to avoid conflict is for her to mark a calendar with a colored pencil, charting her menstrual cycle. This could be a secret sex chart that is mutually shared. Maintaining such a personal chart extends the sexual intimacy and anticipation and prevents not knowing where a woman is on the sexual mood scale.

Remember that when a mate makes himself vulnerable, he is asking for acceptance. If a woman rejects her partner, he may feel frustrated and unloved. It is important for both partners to acknowledge the other's needs and desires. At the same time, however, no one should deny his or her own feelings to please someone else all of the time.

SO MANY DIFFERENCES, SO LITTLE TIME

Another major difference between men and women is the *he* wants action and *she* wants romance. *He* wants intercourse and *she* wants tenderness. *He* wants to look. *She* wants to talk.

Take Charlotte's story, for example. She came to the office on a rainy Monday morning. Charlotte began by relating what had happened that weekend.

Charlotte was very excited on the Saturday of her thirty-fourth birthday. While coloring her long red hair she mentally planned her birthday evening. The new black dress she would wear . . . . What she would order in her favorite restaurant . . . . The beat of the music she and her husband would dance to at their favorite night spot . . . . The birthday jewelry he was certain to give her. All of these thoughts floated deliciously through her mind as she fantasized her birthday celebration.

Bart brought Charlotte long-stemmed red roses. Dinner was exceptionally good. He suggested they forgo the dancing and return home where he would give Charlotte her birthday present. Filled with anticipation, she happily agreed. Once in the living room, Bart presented Charlotte with a large box wrapped with a big red bow. Definitely not jewelry. When Charlotte opened the box and removed the tissue paper she found a luscious black nightgown. Bart urged Charlotte to try on the gown immediately.

> "When I came out wearing the nightgown, Bart gasped his appreciation and told me how sensationally sexy I looked. Then, he picked me up in his arms and immediately started for the bedroom. I don't know why I felt so disappointed, almost empty. I know he had planned a lovely birthday dinner, brought me roses, and given me a beautiful gift. I knew I looked sexy and inviting. Who wouldn't in such a breathtaking gown? Of course Bart would respond in a physical way. What was missing? Why did I feel this way? Why wasn't my response to Bart's lovemaking as intense and satisfying as I would have liked it to have been?"

What had gone wrong? Why didn't Charlotte feel close to Bart on that special evening? It was apparent she needed to get in touch with her emotional and sexual needs.

COMMUNICATING THROUGH CONVERSATION AND TOUCH

Charlotte needs to tell Bart to take the time to stroke her before he begins sexual intercourse. She needs to ask him to gently tell her with both words and touch how really lovely *she* is, not just in the fabulous nightgown. Women need to hear how much they mean to their lovers. When a man responds to his partner without the caresses she so desperately needs to feel loved, not just desired, sex for her often does feel empty.

It is not easy for a woman to tell her mate what she needs to be more sexually responsive. She should not begin this dialogue in the bedroom, but at a time when both partners are relaxed, perhaps on a long drive in the country. Then it should become a part of regular communication between mates. It is important to discuss these feelings in a calm and caring way. Partners need to be in constant sexual conversation with each other, sharing all thoughts, moods, and desires. When couples are so in tune with each other, expressing specific requests during lovemaking does not take on such overwhelming responses. It becomes a natural part of communicating that makes both partners happy.

WHEN SEX SEEMS LIKE A DEMAND, NOT AN EXPRESSION OF LOVE

It is important for a woman to feel as special to her mate as she did the first time they ever made love together, no matter how long they have been together. It is easy for lovers to forget and take each other for granted when they are both involved in the activities of daily living . . . work, children, friends, and family. The lawn must be mowed and the kids must be carpooled. Neither one seems to notice how seldom they spend an evening together . . . alone. Sex is sporadic and infrequent. He barely notices her new dress. She knows he isn't really listening when she relays the day's events. She feels frustrated. Why does she bother? She knows why. She wants him to pay attention to her. She wants him to see her as a complete person before she is willing to be the satisfying sexual partner he desires.

When Susan, thirty-eight and very attractive, and John, forty-two and obviously angry, came into the office, Susan said she felt as though there was nothing else she could do. She and John had been married for seventeen years and had moved so far apart emotionally and sexually, Susan felt certain there was no way they could ever get back together. She was clearly fed up and began the session in a fit of indignation.

"I'm not having oral sex or *any* sex with John! I want someone to court me for a change. Someone to make me feel special. All he wants is a sex machine, and I'm not going to be an object.

"John is a rep for an office supply firm. I have a part-time job as a receptionist for a dentist and take care of our three teenage children. In the years we've been married, John has traveled constantly during the week. He almost never calls me from the road. Then he comes home late on Friday and expects me to give him oral sex. I can't. I won't. I tell him again and again, if he won't do anything for me, why should I do anything for him?"

John also had his side of the story to tell, and it was essential to hear his perspective.

"I am on the road all week long trying to sell to companies who don't want my products. It is so lonely in the evenings in stark hotel rooms. Many days I feel completely worn out and worn down. When I come home, all I want is a little loving. For Susan to give me oral sex feels like the most loving thing she could possibly do. I always thought for a woman to have oral sex meant she was giving all her love. I need that love from Susan. It makes me feel like she wants me, that she can't get enough of me. When Susan says she won't give me oral sex if I won't be romantic first, I don't want to be romantic. I don't feel romantic. I just feel angry."

Susan needs to tell John that for her to feel sexy toward him, she needs to first feel close to him. Close for a woman means talking, touching, and spending time outside of the bedroom. Emotions are what stir the sexual fires for women. Susan needs to be specific with John. She needs to tell him what romantic means to her. A man doesn't know what romantic means to a woman unless she tells him.

MEMORIES ARE SEXUAL TRIGGERS
Couples need to remember what it was like when they first began to care about each other. Susan recalled those early years. "Yes, I remember," she responded rather dreamily. "We planned everything together. I would do anything to please him. I worried about every little expression, every gesture, every word, and wondered what it

meant. My whole being seemed wrapped around what John would do or say."

John remembered saving for her birthday. "We had just started going together. I didn't have this job yet; I worked as a clerk in a men's clothing store and didn't make much money. Susan wanted a cashmere sweater. It was very expensive but I bought it for her anyway. She looked beautiful in that shade of blue."

"I still have that sweater. I remember how thrilled I was that you got it for me. It was the first nice thing I ever had," Susan recollected.

Susan and John agreed they needed to recapture the depth of their initial caring, but they really didn't know how. Susan could start by telling John how much she wants to be shown that he cares for her in words as well as actions. She might ask him to call from the road at night or from the office during the day just to share how things are going. She could tell him how much she would like to find a card on her pillow or a note in the refrigerator telling her how much he loves her. They could plan to go out for a drink when he returns from a business trip and talk.

Apart from that, they need to spend time outside the bedroom. He could come home with a rose or a pretty gift to show he has been thinking of her while he was away. Maybe a poem he clipped from the daily newspaper or a cartoon would have special meaning. When it comes to romance, a woman needs to spell it out for a man, telling him that little things mean a lot.

When Susan tells John her feelings after a downward spiral, she has to do it in a positive, caring way. She shouldn't say, "You always . . ." or, "You never . . ." To say, "In the past twelve years you have never called or remembered" is not useful. It will only hurt and anger John. It would be better for Susan to say gently, "I know you feel angry now. I know you feel hurt and neglected. That is exactly how I feel." But, once she has told him, she doesn't need to keep on telling him. That won't change anything. Remember the ancient definition of insanity. Insanity is doing the same thing over and over and expecting different results.

Susan laughed, but she got the point. She needed to do something different, and she did.

THE BATTLE BETWEEN THE SEXES

As long as human beings have existed, there have been countless discussions about the differences between men and women. Of course, it is often these very differences that cause men and women to be attracted to one another. This lack of understanding between the sexes can cause endless conflict and confusion.

> "I know Sal needs me. He wouldn't last a day without me. Why is he so unable to tell me? All I want is a little appreciation. I tell him all the time how much I admire him. He is rugged and funny and very good in bed. When I say these things to him, he responds by asking, 'If I'm so good in bed, why do you give me such a hard time with sex?'"

This woman, Alicia, was clearly fed up with her feelings of being taken for granted.

> "Sal's idea of sex and mine are completely different. He is happy when he can complete the sex act. A turn-on to him is reading the latest issue of *Hustler* magazine. If I am taking off a slip, he thinks that is an invitation to go to bed with him. I want to have sex with him when he asks about my day and helps me with the dishes. This makes no sense to Sal.
>
> "Every evening, when Sal comes home from work, I greet him with a kiss. At least, I'm expecting a kiss. I usually get a peck on the cheek as he passes me while glancing to see what we're having for dinner. I always ask about his day. His answer is usually something like, 'It was okay.' I have to pump him to get any additional information. I want to know what the people were like on his calls. He is a plumbing contractor. I want Sal to describe their homes to me and tell me what they talked about. He says they don't talk. He is paid by the minute. Customers seldom offer him a cup of coffee. Everyone wants to see him leave so the meter doesn't keep running.
>
> "Our four children are small, so usually they are fed before Sal and I have dinner. They play and watch television, while I try to serve Sal his favorite foods. He is seldom ill, but once last winter he had the flu. I brought him juice and tea until I thought I would drop. All he did was complain about how bad he felt. He was upset when we ran out of orange juice and I gave him apple, saying that his mother would never run out of

oranges. Not once did he express concern that I might get his flu or that I might be exhausted. About two weeks ago, I developed back pain. The doctor told me that I needed to get off my feet. What a joke! How does a mother with four children under eight get off her feet? When I asked Sal to give me a hand with the dishes, he said that's why we have a built-in dishwasher. He suggested I ask my mother to come over to help me change the sheets on the bed. Later, when he wanted sex, I refused. Not only did my back hurt and I felt his request was insensitive, I was really turned off when I passed the bedroom to see him reading *Playboy* on the bed.

"I know, in my heart of hearts, that Sal really loves me. I provide a loving home where he can relax and let down his guard against that hostile world out there. Although ours might be a traditional marriage in this modern day and age, I am very proud that it is. I suppose I am one of those rare women who really loves being a homemaker. Although I do complain, there is nothing in life I would rather do than provide a nurturing atmosphere for my children and Sal. I do like sex with Sal. It has always been good between us sexually. It is just that when he acts so insensitively to my needs, I feel the only way I can make him aware of how I feel is to withhold sex from him for a while. This is punishing us both. I need some constructive help to bridge the gap of the obvious differences between us."

Although nurturing was her strong suit, Alicia wanted her value to Sal reaffirmed in words, not with sex. One major difference between men and women is that men are generally action-oriented while women generally crave conversation. Women are centered on the person. Men are centered on things. Women need to feel love to have sex. Men believe they are showing love when they initiate sex. When couples disagree, a woman usually wants to resolve the disagreement so that she can feel closer to her mate. Men avoid confrontation at all cost. Most feel if they tend to bring home a paycheck and take out the garbage, there should be no reason for conflict.

Although it will be difficult, Alicia needs to convince Sal that partners can learn from each other's thoughts and ideas. She needs to tell Sal that when her emotions and feelings about his behavior toward her are overlooked, she feels he doesn't care. Alicia needs to ask Sal to listen to her, and then to respond verbally. He might think this is both silly and impossible, at first. But, as Alicia reported in her therapy session, Sal does love her as much as she loves him. If she is able to ask him to respect her feelings, no matter how inconsequential he might feel they are, that will go a long way toward making her want to be intimate with him.

Alicia might try to develop a sense of humor about some of the habits Sal will probably be unable to break. She needs to ask herself, how important is it that he change a particular behavior? Does this offending habit really affect the relationship? Or, is it just something minor that irritates her? If Alicia is aware that what is bothering her is very minor, she needs to ask herself, "Why does it bother me so much?" It may be she is expecting Sal to fulfill some unrealistic expectations. Maybe the things Sal does to offend Alicia are done for the same reason she is withholding sex from him. He may want her attention. He might want Alicia to hear about some of her habits that irritate him.

Alicia expresses a generosity of spirit in providing for Sal's comforts in the home. Perhaps she needs to reinforce her knowledge of Sal's accomplishments outside the house. He tells her she does not understand the nature of his work day. He also does not try to explain it to her. These hours make up a significant part of the missing puzzle of his life. Sal needs to include Alicia in social intercourse as well as physical. Sharing and talking are what communication is all about. Men and women have different modes of operating. Partners need to understand and appreciate what these differences are. Antagonism over both trivial and meaningful acts needs to be resolved on an on-going basis so that these negative feeling do not interfere with a couple's sex life. A partner who is complacent about responding to another partner's needs is much more likely to ensure long-standing marital difficulties in the relationship. When partners are able to recognize gender differences, and accept them as important without expecting a partner to change them, mates have a much better opportunity to be fulfilling sexual partners who enrich the relationship. No one way is the right way. Each partner's perspective is different. As the saying goes, "Different is good."

SO MUCH TIME; SO LITTLE REWARD

"I first met Terry when he appeared as the guest speaker for my company's annual meeting. I appeared calm and in control, I'm certain, but inwardly I was feeling very nervous when I directed Terry to the speaker's table on that hectic Spring day. I could actually feel him staring at my legs as I led him down the hotel hallway at a brisk clip. I enjoyed that feeling. His eyes seemed to burn through the tailored business suit I had chosen to wear to that momentous meeting. I experienced an overwhelming desire to have him loosen my barrette and run his fingers through my hair with wild abandon. His manner was very intense. It excited me, I confess. I wondered what it would be like to be with him in a different setting . . . say a candlelit dinner for two later in the hotel dining room. I could visualize lying nude together on a white bearskin rug in front of a fireplace somewhere. I didn't care where.

"These were unusual feelings for me to have. I am considered by all who know me to be very cool and efficient. I have spent years cultivating this demeanor. I work long hours and have studied diligently to secure a key role in the future of my company. My life is so concentrated on my profession, I've had little opportunity to meet men. Terry had such an unexpected effect on me, I found myself wondering, for the first time in years, what it would be like to be married to such a man.

"After the annual meeting, when everyone had exchanged thank yous and farewells, Terry asked me to join him for a drink in the hotel bar. Pleading work, I declined. That seemed to only add to his desire to see me again. That old ploy of being unavailable really works, I thought to myself. When he asked me to join him for dinner later, I was delighted. I readily accepted his invitation to remain downtown and join him for dinner.

"It was surprising we had never met before. Our interests in music and art were similar. Terry enjoyed sports and so did I. We shared a few mutual friends and a strong desire to be nationally recognized in our field. It was interesting to me that I did not feel competitive with Terry when I shared some of my ideas. He was open and eager to expand on what he thought were great perceptions.

"Seven months later, we were enjoying a torrid love affair. I had never felt so vibrant. So alive! When we were not working, all our waking moments were spent together. We even found a way to collaborate on an ad campaign that made money for both our firms and won us a national award. Marriage was alluded to on rare occasions. But I did find myself thinking more and more about a house in the suburbs and children playing in the yard.

"Terry seemed as ecstatic about our relationship as I. He told me time and time again that he never thought he would meet a woman who was as totally independent and successful as he. Dependent women, he told me, really turned him off. He relished the fact that I really did not need his guidance or his bank account. I cherished that mutual excitement. When Terry told me I was a wonderful, caring lover who demanded no commitment beyond the joy of being together for as long as these feelings remained, I did begin to feel a little concerned.

"That first Christmas of our romance, my parents invited Terry to join us for church and dinner on Christmas Eve. Terry resisted, saying he disliked the idea of attending church and my family looking him over. I was very surprised and extremely hurt at his response. I thought of us as a couple and I assumed Terry did as well. I felt too emotionally involved to risk the thought of spending the holidays alone if I confronted Terry with my feelings. So, I told my family I would not be joining them this year.

"My anger and resentment seemed to increase as New Year's Eve approached. Two days before, I asked Terry where this relationship was going. I was devastated when he told me he was not ready for marriage. I felt used and betrayed. I ended the affair that evening. I have absolutely no idea how to turn this wonderful love affair into a lifetime commitment."

BUSINESS OR PLEASURE?

If Ruth's affair with Terry had been a business venture, she would never have let this situation continue without establishing partners' goals. Of course, it is difficult to be as clear-headed in a personal relationship as in a business transaction, but some of the same rules do apply. Ruth needed to tell Terry that she did have *some* expectations. Pretending that she didn't was being dishonest with herself and her partner. It is not too late to explain exactly what her feelings are.

It is necessary for Terry *and* Ruth to understand that no one does all the giving all the time in a relationship. Every partner has expectations, whether expressed or not. It is unrealistic for Ruth to think that Terry would reward her for "being so good" with a proposal of marriage. If that was all it took, how could he not consider a long-term commitment with her? Because Ruth had made no demands on him, there was almost no need, beyond the totally altruistic, for Terry to be concerned about Ruth's needs and desires. He continued to be interested in only his own. Ruth needs to tell Terry exactly what her desires are. She needs to express them gently and lovingly. She cannot expect Terry to be a mind reader, but after she has told him how she feels, she should be prepared for him to make up his own mind.

Pretending to want what a partner wants is dishonest and always leads to difficulties. Ruth was misleading Terry by trying to make him believe that she wanted exactly what he did from their relationship. It is essential for a partner to convey with both words and actions his or her needs for future happiness both in and out of the bedroom. Honesty is essential to successful communication.

Perception is often different between the sexes. A partner should never leave what the other might be thinking to chance. Ruth needs to tell Terry that the only thing she desires from him in return for the pleasure of her voluptuous, endearing, charming self is his total commitment for marriage! He can take it or leave it. If he leaves it, at least she won't feel she has been taken advantage of.

TALK ABOUT YOUR DIFFERENCES

While there are countless differences between men and women, the scenarios just described illustrate how important it is to determine exactly what those differences are and discuss them with a partner in a loving, caring way. Many times, even when partners do know exactly what is bothering them, mates are afraid or unsure of how to tell a significant other. Because people tend to react strongly to rejection, it is necessary to explain the problem while making very clear it is not one partner's fault. Because mates do love one another, partners should express clearly their desire to overcome or change the situation. However, words can escape many lovers while under emotional stress. When partners reassure each other that they have the relationship's best interests at heart, the words themselves become less important than the loving tone and manner with which they are conveyed. Remember, there were few words used in the backseat. It was the feelings that made it better.

CHAPTER 2

Speak to Me of Love, Not Bills

Foreplay is a twenty-four-hour-a-day affair for most women, in that it is everything that happens between partners during the day. This is often difficult for a man to understand. For a woman, foreplay begins when the couple awakens in the morning. From that moment on, everything her partner says and everything her partner does affects how she will feel sexually throughout the day. It is absolutely true that the majority of women need romance. Every survey on record supports these findings. According to Ann Lander's survey of 90,000 women, 72 percent prefer to be held closely and treated tenderly rather than have actual intercourse. "If you read poetry to me or take a walk with me, holding hands, I may have oral sex with you," many women say. But, as one male asked, "What does poetry have to do with oral sex?"

Women need help changing roles required of them throughout the course of a day. Since romance does help a woman feel loved, and feeling loved helps her feel sexual, there are numerous steps couples can take to create romance in their relationship. One excellent example is the case of Mary.

> "*Jeeze*, Mary, I can't *believe* you've overdrawn our checking account *again*! Don't you keep track of the checks you write? Don't you *know* this will cost us money? *Jeeze*."

The deep voice emanating from the small woman sitting in the chair opposite me startled me at first, and then made me laugh.

Mary was imitating the way her husband spoke to her that made her feel infuriated and infantile.

"Roger makes me feel so incompetent. He is always yelling at me about something, and then, later, in our bedroom, wonders why I don't want to have sex with him. What I really want to do is *hit* him. I certainly don't feel very sensual when he hollers at me like that. He is always upset over bills and money. Doesn't he realize I don't make mistakes on purpose? I'm busy, too. I do my best. What makes him have this power over me?"

Of course, Mary was giving Roger the power over her feelings. No one person has the power to *make* someone else feel something. Overdrawing the checking account is something anyone can learn to control by recording the checks more carefully. Mary continued to describe other incidents that left her feeling inadequate.

"I can do nothing right! If I make pasta for dinner, he had it for lunch. If I get the house clean but the kids' toys are scattered all over the family room, he yells that I am not a good housekeeper. If I have a meeting in the evening and I ask Roger to put our two toddlers to bed, he complains because *he* has had a long hard day at work. What does he think I do all day? We always seem to go to bed angry with each other, and don't tell me you should never do that. How can I feel loving toward him when I am filled with animosity? How can I resolve these constant feelings of resentment toward Roger so that I can respond to him sexually? I'd like to have some passionate feelings of my own that don't involve murder. I want and need some love and sex. Why doesn't his anger affect *his* sexual feelings?"

Men are very different than women in this way. Men's sexual desire seems so much less dependent on outside influences, whereas women respond more strongly to the atmosphere around them. A woman has a hundred things that need to be "right" before she can have sex. Very little seems to detract a man from wanting to make love. Because many couples are unaware of these discrepancies between men and women, on-going communication between two partners becomes very important.

It can be very empowering for couples if each partner tries to *think of love as a verb.* Something you *do.* Not something you *get.* When partners love each other, it is natural to want to please a mate, as well as wish to be pleased in return. But, as long as a partner's behavior is a *condition* for whether or not to give love, that love cannot be given freely. Mary needs to try giving her affection unconditionally, because she loves Roger. Although it may be difficult for Mary to think positive thoughts about Roger when he's criticizing her, she can try to block out his words and overcome her negative feelings with positive ones. Mary needs to show Roger her love in spite of what he is saying. This will probably change Roger's attitude and behavior toward her almost immediately. Roger needs to also love Mary unconditionally—whether or not the house is clean and the checkbook balanced. Only through this unconditional love will the lines of communication be opened.

Couples can drastically improve their relationship by putting their love into action. Once they do this, everything else seems to follow more easily.

"How can you give your love to your partner when you are furious with the way he is treating you?" Mary asked. This is an excellent question. It is not easy. It takes insight. Partners must constantly remind themselves of all the good and pleasant things in their lives together. Mary needs to let go of the momentary "resentment" she has against Roger, focus on the love, and try not to get too caught up in his criticism. When she is away from Roger, Mary needs to recall the things she loved about him in the very beginning of their relationship.

> "I thought Roger was the best looking hunk I ever saw. He was so thoughtful. I remember on our second date he brought me daisies from a street vendor because I told him about picking daisies as a child on my grandfather's farm. He remembered. It was all those little things, helping me with my coat, opening the car door. He liked to do things for me and help me in funny ways. Once he tried to carry a bookcase we bought at an auction up to my apartment and it got stuck in the elevator. We laughed so hard we had to sit down on the floor. The bookcase

got scratched, but Roger just took my can opener out of the kitchen drawer and scratched it some more and said I should tell people it was distressed wood. Now he is just a demanding perfectionist who is never satisfied. We don't laugh together when things go wrong like we used to."

RECAPTURE THE MAGIC

Mary should tell Roger how she remembers those wonderful qualities about him. She is certain to think of many others as she recaptures their courtship and the early years of their marriage. Mary and Roger can spend time together alone, reminiscing about when they first made love or how they acquired some of their more "interesting" pieces of furniture. Sharing such memories over a glass of wine after the children are in bed seems to work for many couples.

Roger is worried about money. Mary can make a serious effort not to run up bills or overdraw her checking account. Perhaps she could ask Roger to help her manage her accounting more effectively. She could suggest they set aside a few minutes on Thursday evenings, after the kids are in bed, to go over the household bills. If improving Mary's budgetary skills is too stressful a task for them to manage together at this time, Mary could go to a financial advisor for an hour or two on her own and learn how to better handle money. Since it is *her* problem, she will have to find the solution, unless she wants Roger to go on yelling about her mismanagement.

It is much easier for a partner to overlook a mate's faults when that person is working hard to overcome them. This couple's house is not in perfect order. Whose is? Especially with small children living there, priorities need to be determined. What is more important to this couple? A spotless home with no energy left for joy and sexual abandon because the wife is too exhausted at the end of the day? Or, a mess in the family room as a couple races to get the kids to bed so the partners can wrestle between the sheets in disorderly fashion in their bedroom? Life is a series of choices. Mary can explain to Roger that when he constantly criticizes her, he spoils her appetite for sex. She can tell him she wants to be with him and ask him to save his criticism for a note he could write and leave on the kitchen counter for her to read after her morning cup of coffee. Something like this perhaps:

> *Dear Mary,*
> *I would appreciate you picking up the kids' toys before I get home, because if I break my neck, I will be unable to make wild passionate love to you later in bed. Broken bones really inhibit my sexual performance.*
>
> *Love, Roger*

Who could be angry with a note like that? And, look at what they both have to look forward to in private moments when they are able to trust that a partner's anger and disappointment will be conveyed in a loving manner.

Mary and Roger could also keep a secret sex chart for each other. If he helps put the kids to bed, he gets a star. His prize could be a special sexual toy, an erotic video, or a video camera so they can make their own. If Mary gets the star for something she has done that Roger wants, her prize might be a beautiful piece of sexy lingerie, some perfume, or, her back rubbed . . . either way, both receive the reward. Everyone wants to be appreciated. Partners need to instigate ideas to show that they treasure each other in ways that are fun and exciting for both people in the relationship.

Mary can ask Roger to call her during the day. They can plan what they will do together when Roger gets home. Mary should tell him she needs to feel his care and concern. Mary needs for Roger to make her feel like she is his number one priority. It is important for Roger to handle his customers with the greatest sensitivity in his business relationships. Mary can remind Roger that she is his most important client in his personal life. Mary should let him know (with a twinkle in her eye) that she wants to *buy* what he has to *sell!* She could also suggest that a little help with the housework goes further in making her want to please him in the bedroom than all of his lectures about her shortcomings.

When Mary realized how much fun this could all be, she was able to tell Roger what she needed (and didn't need) in the spirit of play. Roger loved the zest she showed in wanting to please him. He respected the fact that Mary did not want to be criticized if she fell short of his expectations. It did not take long for Roger to realize that caring and praise go further in the bedroom than demands and criticism ever could.

When a woman is able to tell her mate what she wants him to know both clearly and lovingly, they will be better able to live a life filled with verve, exuberance, and mutual satisfaction. Sex will become an enjoyable expectation for them both.

SMALL IRRITATIONS CAN CAUSE BIG PROBLEMS

Little things? True. But it is the little things people often overlook in their hectic lives. Couples, in their scramble for achievement, often forget the romance that is so badly needed for a woman to feel sexual. If a woman does not feel sexual, she will usually say no. This is one situation where "just say no!" is not effective.

When bills, septic tanks, children, and in-laws become the focus of a couple's conversation, sexual feelings toward a partner will certainly diminish. Remember what made you feel passionate toward your partner in the beginning of your relationship? It was that each of you was the other's all-consuming interest. As busy and goal-oriented as you were, your prime concern was your lover. You called during the day. He brought you a flower. You walked in the woods holding hands. You went dancing and had quiet dinners together or picnics in the park. Your lover was the one person you wanted to talk to and you shared every thought and experience that happened when you were not together. You trusted your partner completely and knew that there would be total understanding and acceptance.

Most women still need that attention in order to feel loved. When a woman feels loved, she gives love. She wants her mate to give her the same consideration he would his most valued client. Sometimes, when a woman is able to explain to her man in this context, one he uses every day, a man is able to understand her more completely. In the business world, he perceives the needs and concerns of the person he is trying to persuade to buy his product or service. When he learns those needs, he tries to fill them. A man needs to listen attentively to a woman's needs and concerns and attend to those needs with all the loving care he possesses. He will be amazed at the reward!

Kelly and Mark had been lovers for seven years before they married. Kelly was a very successful real estate agent. Her effervescent personality caught Mark's attention the first time he saw her. Kelly was at her best when closing a deal. The excitement of her bustling life agreed with her. Mark, a title agent, fully understood what it took to be at the top in her field. He felt a great pride in Kelly's drive and business ability. He loved her free spirit.

When they married, it was no surprise to anyone. No one doubted they would continue to live a fun-loving, high-spirited life together. Each was completely independent financially. They loved work. They shared most of their friends and supported each other's outside interests. What, then, was Kelly doing in a therapist's office some ten months later?

> "Our sex life is horrible! It used to be so exhilarating and unpredictable. Mark was a wonderful, inventive, caring lover. I could never get enough of him. Now, it is like having sex by rote. His moves are so predictable. He is obsessed by our house. I hate it! What happened to us?"

Kelly went on to describe their past seven years together.

> "Well, Mark and I each had our own condos in the same complex. Mine was all white. The carpet and walls and couches were done in soft white. Even the kitchen was uncluttered and sophisticated, all done in black and white. I had chosen white wicker furniture for the bedroom. The only other colorful objects were red velvet pillows on the bed and a fantastic floral oil which hung over the buffet in the dining room. It was a beautiful condo. I loved it.
>
> "Mark's home was very masculine . . . tweeds and leather. It looked just like him. We used to prepare wonderful dinners there. Often we never made it to dessert. We would spend hours on the floor in front of his fireplace, making love or dreamily planning our life together. We plotted exotic vacations in foreign lands. Mark has a unique ability to make almost any situation

erotic. He delights in surprising me and I'm always up for it. That is, he used to be that way, until these past few months.

"Mark and I bought a lovely home in Rolling Acres, the new development at the edge of town. We have a garden and a small pool, and there is a jacuzzi off the master bedroom. We sold our condos and combined our assets."

As Kelly began to describe the decor, the changes in the sexual atmosphere became apparent.

"My white furniture is in the living room. It's a little barren looking in this setting. The wicker furniture is in the guest bedroom. We put Mark's leather chair in the den, but his couch was so worn, we're going to buy a new one. I want chintz, but he likes leather, so we will have to work that out when the time comes.

"We used to have many sexual rendezvous in the kitchen, but this kitchen is not going to get messed up! I have to clean it! I have a place for everything, even my spices. It really aggravates me when Mark wants to leave everything just as it is and head for the bedroom. He doesn't seem to realize I can't stand the mess. I'm the one who has to clean it up later. Every time I buy something new for the house, he has a fit. I find all these little touches make a home. They are really not extravagances. After all, I pay half the bills.

"Our bedroom is really beautiful. We chose the furniture together. The four poster bed has a canopy and is so high off the floor you need a step stool to get in. The dressers are massive, but the room can take it. There is a large fern in the window between two brocaded chairs. It looks just like a page out of *Architectural Digest*.

"But with all this beauty, there is no romance. That is the problem. Septic tanks! That is what we talk about. Our septic tank and the mulch. Yes. Mulch. Honest. While I am gazing admiringly around the room, Mark lies there absentmindedly stroking my body going on and on about our compost heap. It's really a turn-off, I can tell you. I know he's never had a house of his own before, but this is really ridiculous."

Kelly desperately wanted to restore their sex life to the stimulating passion they once shared. She understood that her husband was enthralled with his new surroundings, as was she, but she did not know how to get the conversation out of the compost heap.

MEMORIES ARE MADE OF THIS

All relationships are built by memories. It is clear that Kelly and Mark had erased the environmental memories that triggered their erotic impulses . . . the intoxicating smells and tastes that accompanied sex in the kitchen, the lazy lovemaking on Mark's worn couch in the den, the reckless abandon of wild love in the wicker rocker. All these were gone, replaced by beautiful but sterile surroundings in which their personal lives had yet to evolve.

Although most people have a lot on their minds, whether it be unresolved conflict from business life or annoying household concerns like building a compost heap, these problems have no place in the bedroom. A woman needs to feel she is the most important thing in her man's life. She wants to feel that when he is making love to her, there is nothing else on his mind except her. Anything less is a turn-off.

Couples need to determine what their priorities are. If what they want is a picture-perfect house, then they will have to forego the spontaneous, all-consuming lovemaking they enjoyed in the past. Sex is messy. If you take the time to pick everything up along the way and your mind is on the cover shot of *House Beautiful*, then your thoughts can't be totally on your partner. Your concentration is broken and the momentum is gone. Loving partners need to make a choice, and proceed from there.

When Kelly arrived for her next appointment, she had decided she would do everything she could to bring the old Mark back.

> "I served dinner on the floor on a blanket in front of the fireplace in our new den last night. Although the chicken was sticky and the wine got spilled, it was the best sex we've had in months! I hired a cleaning crew today to come in once a week. If we have nights like that, it is worth the expense. But, I still need help with the compost heap!"

Now that Kelly has moved sex from the difficult surroundings of their formal bedroom to the more familiar ones of the kitchen and the floor of the family room, it is time for her to tell Mark how she feels about his conversation and lack of attention when they are together in bed.

Kelly could explain that she understands being a homeowner is new and perplexing to Mark and that she appreciates his concern. He needs to know one of the things she loves about him is his ability to take care of things. But, in the bedroom, the only thing they need to discuss is taking care of one another.

This couple needs to establish new memories in their new surroundings. First, they can do something to make their bedroom more conducive to making love. They can install mirrors along the wall or above the bed. Replacing paisley sheets with satin and returning those red velvet pillows to their rightful place of honor on the four poster bed can add spice to a bland room. Kelly can do the unexpected like wearing something erotic and giving him some sensuous article of clothing to wear as well. She needs to create a new enticing arena of love. This ingenuity that Kelly so admired in Mark will be rekindled when he sees how passionate she is in her desire to seduce him in their new environment.

Kelly could tactfully suggest that they change their pillow talk from compost heaps to how each of them could excite the other. Planning sexual games together in bed, talking about what they propose to do *to* and *for* each other will constantly keep each of them turned on and full of expectation. This can be great fun for a couple.

Since they are in a new home, they can videotape making love in each new room in different ways. All the magazines feature accessories to update a house. Kelly and Mark could become their own accessory! Not only will this action put new zest into their sex life, they will have the video to excite them when they feel they want a less ambitious turn-on. This 'hobby' can go on for years as they 're-decorate.' It will certainly give Mark and Kelly something much more interesting to talk about in bed than their compost heap.

FORTY ISN'T FUNNY

Many men and women feel they will not survive the trauma of a landmark birthday like forty. To many, these events symbolize the end of youth and along with it the passion of living. Particularly at this time, it is natural for mates to yearn for sex to be as exciting as it was initially. The truth is, what seemed exhilarating at twenty and inventive at thirty may feel uncomfortable at forty. Both men and women have difficulty in seeing their bodies change. At this time, a partner may question his or her sexuality and imagine the other partner must feel the same. Many fail to appreciate that the shared experience of these subtle changes can enhance and deepen sexual commitment and enjoyment far into the golden years.

"I will never forget the morning of my fortieth birthday. Last Friday was the day I had been dreading for months. My husband and family had been teasing me that I was afraid of leaving my youth behind when the big 40 appeared on my calendar. They were right! I think almost every woman imagines she will wake up fat or wrinkled on her fortieth birthday. Of course, what I was really afraid of was sexual rejection. Aren't most women when they turn forty?

"Well, anyway, I thought my hair looked great when I used to wear it long and permed. Now, the style seemed juvenile and unsophisticated to me. I didn't want to be one of those women who looks like she is trying to hang on to her youth. I also didn't want to lose my femininity and my sex appeal. Even my wardrobe of comfortable jeans and T-shirts seemed inappropriate and more appropriate for my daughters. So, I gave it all away to charity.

"Logical or not, this is a very difficult time for me. Unrealistic as it may seem, I feel I have just a few short years left and I need to pack everything into them that I can. I don't think there is a woman alive who does not experience feelings of panic and insecurity when she reaches forty. How can I compete with all those younger women out there? They all look so vital and gorgeous. I see my husband eyeing them, even though he pretends he is not. All *we* seem to talk about is planning for the girls' college and saving money for our retirement. Marty's behavior makes me feel even older than I am. I don't want to be so serious all the time. I want to have fun. Why should one birthday do so much to change my life? Is my sex life over?"

TAKE BACK YOUR PEARLS

"Carol, What makes you think your sex life with your husband is over just because you've had a fortieth birthday? What happened on the morning of your birthday that sent you for counseling?" I asked.

"Marty gave me pearls," came the unexpected response.

"What's wrong with pearls? That's a lovely gift," I responded. But this response prompted Carol to express a lot of the feelings that had been building up recently. "It's a lovely gift . . . for a bride or a new mother. I wanted him to give me something that showed he still thought of me as an erotic, exciting woman. By giving me his grandmother's pearls, Marty was saying he sees me as someone ethereal and motherly. He also didn't have to spend any money. I know that sounds mean, but, I wanted him to do something extravagant for a change. I wanted Marty to buy me something romantic and impractical to tell me I was still exciting at forty. I wanted him to see me as a sexually vibrant woman who deserved a sensationally romantic present.

"When Marty and I first married, we were both recently graduated from the university we attended on partial scholarship. Our student loans were enormous and took us many years to repay. I got a job immediately as the marketing director for a nonprofit organization. The salary wasn't great, but it did pay for our small apartment and the groceries. Marty went on to graduate school to receive his doctorate in economics. He is a successful stockbroker today, and we live very comfortably. Our two children have lacked for very little. But Marty always talks about money.

"Our sex life has never been that exciting, but it has always been comfortable. Last year, a group of women in my investment group took a weekend trip to Chicago to attend a seminar. The members of this investment group are primarily wives of other stockbrokers with whom Marty is associated. We wives decided to form this group so that we would have a better idea of what our husbands are talking about. We also wanted to make a little money of our own to spend on things we wanted, but felt we couldn't afford out of the household budget.

"Attending that seminar turned out to be more like a sorority weekend. We were all giddy. It was wonderful being released from the usual routine of housewives and mothers. We did a little window shopping between sessions and I decided to have my hair cut. We ordered drinks before dinner on Saturday night. Perhaps it was the alcohol and unfamiliar surroundings that really seemed to loosen our tongues, but the conversation turned to sex almost immediately.

"This was a new experience for me. I had never discussed my sex life, not even with my closest friends. Among these women, with whom I was only casually acquainted, discussing orgasms, penis size, PMS, and sexual boredom seemed completely natural. It was an exhilarating and informative weekend for me. I must confess, my memories are much clearer about the sexual information exchanged than the discussions of mutual funds at the seminar.

"There were five of us sharing two bedrooms and our sex talk went on into the night. We were all equally enthusiastic about sharing information and our mutual frustrations. It was the first time I realized my secret sexual desires were not unusual. It was clear not one of us was certain her feelings were normal. Our sexual sharing served as a validation of our mutual disappointments and unmet needs. The honesty itself was freeing. One of the women actually described her husband as a groping, sexual clod in bed. When asked why she still stayed with him, she replied she didn't think anyone else would be much better.

"After this enlightening weekend of sharing sexual behavior openly with four other women, I began to read almost every new book the library stocked on sexual relationships. What bothered me the most was that they all seemed to stress the importance of maintaining beautiful, athletic bodies and strong sexual appetites. I had neither. Although I am not fat, I am big-boned. My dress size was a ten at the time. It did not make me feel any better to read that today's size ten is yesterday's size twelve, downsized for marketing purposes. I am aware that no calendar artist would choose me as his subject, in spite of this newfound knowledge about marketing trends. My body was one I tried to disguise by wearing black dresses and long, tunic sweaters. A sweatshirt over jeans with an elasticized waistband was my favorite attire. On the infrequent occasions when Marty and I did make love, I prefer the bedroom to be darkened and the covers to be over me, even in the summer.

"Marty is no Adonis either. Years of making homemade beer in the basement with his buddies has taken its toll on his physique, too. I guess I can assume some of the blame because I am always forcing an extra piece of my less-than-famous apple pie on him after Sunday dinners. Sex between us has become almost ritualized. I know what he will touch where and he knows how I will respond. When it is over, we usually remind each other of something we need to do for the girls or discuss plans for the weekend before we roll over and go to sleep. It's not very exciting. Just comfortable.

"Ten months before my fortieth birthday, I joined a health club. What a struggle. I don't care how easy they say it is. But, I did it. I lost twenty-five pounds, cut off my perm, and purchased a new wardrobe. Everything I bought was black. It is amazing how much fun it is to buy clothes in black when you don't need to hide anything. I even bought three new sexy nightgowns for myself. Marty has only seen two. I was saving the third for what I thought would be my birthday surprise. Now that I have turned forty, I am beginning to realize there are just a few good years left. My children need me less now. I want to have some fun before I lose my looks completely. I don't want to hear about college scholarship tests and car repairs when we are in bed. I feel the years are suddenly rushing away and I'd better make the most of them.

"I know I mentioned money has never been in excess around our house, but we do live comfortably. Marty and I have talked about a trip to Paris for years. It was something we promised ourselves someday. I have dreamed of walking hand-in-hand down the Champs Elysées and floating on a barge down the Seine. I was hoping Marty would surprise me with this romantic second honeymoon for my fortieth birthday. Instead, I awoke to find a faded blue velvet box on my pillow. There stood Marty, grinning in his old terry cloth bathrobe with the torn cuff. 'Open it,' he urged. I did. Inside were his grandmother's pearls. I know I should be thrilled. They were her most valued possession. I would love to have each of our daughters wear them on her wedding day. But, on this last stab at my fleeting youth, I wanted Marty to buy me something frivolous.

"Maybe we couldn't afford a trip to Paris, but I wanted a romantic rendezvous with my husband. I would have been excited with a trip to New York, eating at fabulous restaurants and attending the theater where we could create some lasting romantic memories. Of course, I wouldn't hurt Marty for the world. I acted surprised, which I was, and pleased, which I wasn't. When a couple is practical all of their married life, is it so terrible for a woman to want something romantic and youth-affirming for her fortieth birthday?"

Almost any woman can relate to Carol's feelings of disappointment, unrealistic as it may be to expect a partner's behavior to change completely because of a landmark birthday. Carol believed a romantic trip to Paris would stimulate their stagnant sex life from mundane to inspiring. Carol thought a vacation would relieve the boredom that she was keenly feeling now that she had more time and less financial pressure. Like many mates, Carol did not realize that a difference in atmosphere alone cannot change a couple's sex life entirely. How many people have sought therapy after a disappointing second honeymoon trip? The problem was that Carol had not communicated her very real inner feelings. Marty could not read her mind, so he could not understand that Carol felt terror in reaching this milestone birthday. Carol expected Marty to realize that because she had lost weight and purchased a new wardrobe, she was now interested in an exciting sex life together. These events did not equate in her partner's mind.

It would be possible for Carol to give Marty the trip to Paris for her birthday. Money was shared equally in their marriage, if, albeit, not very often. They did decide together on how income was to be spent. It would not be advisable for Carol to purchase the tickets without discussing the trip with Marty first. But, Carol could explain to Marty how much she wished for them to share this once-in-a-lifetime experience. If future college expenses for their two girls were perceived as overwhelming, this couple could discuss an alternative holiday. The romantic trip in itself was not what was important to Carol.

The real problem was not what Marty had chosen to give Carol for her birthday. Carol was experiencing difficulty in aging. Youth is usually taken for granted. Who was it that said youth is wasted on the young? Sudden realization of the passing years is not an unusual plight for both men and women. Sometimes mid-life crisis, as it is often called, causes a partner to seek other outlets. Some enter into affairs, thinking a new lover will create the sexual excitement currently absent from a relationship. Men have been known to buy a toupee for a receding hairline. Women diet, as did Carol, color their hair, and take up roller-blading or some other youth-oriented activity. All of these endeavors are efforts made to convince partners and themselves that they are really lovable. The overwhelming reason for discontent, whether perceived or not, is that every person needs to feel loved. Therefore, any expression or gift given by a partner is received as an affirmation of that love.

If Marty and Carol are able to discuss what Carol is feeling, they will probably find that each partner has similar needs. Carol might realize that she was looking for that expression of love to be fulfilled in a romantic trip or an extravagant birthday present. Marty might decide to tell Carol he would like her to show him that she still finds him attractive and lovable in spite of his beer belly and torn terry cloth robe. Communication about what each partner needs and wants will make it possible for partners to understand that foreplay is still needed at forty, and even beyond.

THE DEFINITION OF COMMUNICATION IS OFTEN UNCLEAR
People hear so much about communication. But few couples really understand what communication means. Communication means *listening* to what your partner has to say, *hearing* what your partner needs, then, *helping each other* to meet those needs. It is difficult to tell your partner what you want him to know in a way he can hear without resentment. When these words are not accusatory or hostile, but rather, concerned and caring, partners are usually able to communicate very effectively to each other without rancor. More often than not, a mate is able to hear those needs and act on them accordingly. Couples are then able to resolve differences *together*.

It is *the combined action* that seems to make the difference. Each is in control. Each feels *empowered*. After all, the main thing is these couples *want* to give love to and receive love from each other. Satisfaction within the marriage is the primary concern. Overwhelming past experience can cloud the way to a bright, interesting, compassionate future. Learning how to communicate with one another makes it possible to enjoy a more loving relationship together, no matter what the age.

CHAPTER 3

Want Me, Don't Knead Me

Women often complain that their mates grab, poke, and pinch their body parts both in public and in private. A partner may feel he is expressing love and affection, but the woman feels real discomfort or pain. The way a man touches his lover has a great effect on the sexual responsiveness of his mate. Kissing may be a thing of the past for many couples, although the majority of women do report that kissing tends to be very sensual and romantic for them. A moan from a partner can mean either pain or pleasure. One female client reported she moaned every time her husband blew in her ear. Her moans were of discomfort, not of ecstasy. He never knew she had an ear problem and thought that she enjoyed his foreplay.

Couples can use sensate focus techniques to teach pleasurable touch. Formulated by Masters and Johnson, it is something that couples read about constantly but most partners seldom understand. Sensate focusing means learning how to touch and caress each other's bodies without having intercourse. There are some wonderful specific techniques offered in Helen Kaplan's book, *The Illustrated Manual of Sex Therapy*. This is an important part of sexual coupling recommended for all partners to share.

Couples can learn about the likes and dislikes of their mates through these communication skills. Many hours are involved in helping partners better communicate in a loving, caring way. Communication is a real skill that needs to be learned. The results often make the difference between "waiting for it to be over" and enjoying truly satisfying lovemaking with your partner.

When Kate came to therapy for the first time, she was dressed in a tight-fitting sweater and short navy skirt, and looked appealing and sexually self-assured. But she was obviously frightened and a little embarrassed.

"I feel like a fraud. Every time Harry makes love to me, I act as though it is wonderful. But, actually, I cringe when he begins to caress me. When he touches my breasts, it feels like he is trying to knead bread. Sometimes he even pinches my nipples and that hurts a lot. He seems to find one place on my body and rubs and rubs, like he is trying to get out a spot. It excites him when I moan. He doesn't know that I am moaning in pain, and I don't have the heart to tell him.

"When Harry and I first met, I was immediately attracted to him. He was a buyer for a large retail chain of well known women's apparel. I was the manager of a small women's clothing store in a small town in Indiana. My education was completed with my high school graduation ceremony. Harry spoke so well. It was obvious he had been to college. He treated me with great respect and did not make fun of me when I thought the troop withdrawal in the Far East had something to do with sex. Since my graduation, the only man I had dated was Ken who worked at the gas company. He owned a small farm and was planning on settling down there in a few years to raise a family. I never wanted to be a farm wife. Ken would never rise too far at the gas company. Although he was polite and good looking, I had no desire to marry him.

"Harry asked me to dinner at the local tavern. When I accepted, he seemed genuinely pleased. I didn't expect to see him again socially. But the next time he came through on his business trip, he called me first from a neighboring town to see if I would be free that evening. We got along so well. He liked to dance. On one trip, he brought me a yellow felt hat with a red velvet poppy on it. It was darling and he said I looked beguiling in it.

"I was beginning to really care about Harry. He was different. He brought an aura of excitement with him I didn't experience living in my little town. After about six months went by, Harry put a bid on the store where I was working. The owners had been looking to retire and were just waiting for the right offer. Harry has owned the store for about six years now and has become a real pillar in the business community. He is president of a business association and chairman of the United Way for our town. I don't sell dresses anymore. I'm too busy fixing up our new house and taking care of little Bobby, who is three.

"Sex with Harry has always been thrilling to me just because Harry wanted me. When Harry and I first began going together, it seemed as though he was much more gentle. His touch was more tentative then. But, we were exploring, just getting to know each other. He didn't know what would turn me on and what wouldn't.

"I began to fake pleasure with Harry when I realized I had trouble reaching climax. I wanted to prove to Harry I was a real woman. In the beginning, I enjoyed his exploring in places I had never been touched before. We spent leisurely time together. Yes, often in the backseat of his Buick, too. It felt daring and exciting to me to be with this caring, interesting man. Now that we are married, my mind is often on other things when Harry begins to make love to me. I am really not in the same place that he is much of the time. But, I love him and do not want to constantly turn him down when he suggests sex. I feel compelled to perform when he makes love to me. He adores it when I moan. It really turns him on. When he has an orgasm, he thinks I have had one too. To tell him I haven't would make him feel very disappointed with me. I could be satisfied with just sexual play. Satisfied except when it hurts. I've gotten myself into a real dilemma and I don't know how to resolve it."

Kate's plight is one so many women share. Many times a woman is too intimidated to tell her mate what feels good and what does not. Often she is concerned her partner will realize that she has been faking. She can be even more hesitant to tell him something hurts for fear that he might think she is complaining about his lovemaking or she will hurt her partner's ego. When a woman endures her mate's sexual play, very often resentment arises and she will try to avoid sexual contact altogether. This can be very frustrating for both partners.

It is often difficult for a woman to change roles without a great deal of touching and foreplay. She may be under a lot of stress that prohibits the emergence of her sexual feelings . . . problems with the children, her job, her mother . . . the list is endless. Foreplay becomes even more significant to help a woman get into the mood.

When foreplay hurts instead of pleases, it further impedes a woman's sexual responsiveness.

In Kate's case, she needs to explain to Harry, gently, but not in the bedroom, how exciting she finds him and how much she wants to be with him. Then, perhaps over a cup of coffee and his favorite chocolate cake, she could tell him that lately she has noticed some changes in her body. Things that once felt wonderful to her are now giving her discomfort. For example, Kay could tell Harry that she has noticed how much more tender her breasts are than they used to be. She should be certain not to tell him how she has always hated when he touched her in a certain way.

> "This is not going to be easy for me," Kate confided. "I love Harry and I don't want to hurt him, and I certainly don't want him to feel disappointed in me."

Kate needs to reinforce her awareness of her value as a loving, caring, human being. When a woman values herself and is secure in her feelings, she realizes how *she* feels is just as important as how her partner feels. If Harry knew he was hurting her, of course, he would not continue to do so. Kate needs to become aware of other exciting ways she wishes to be touched that will help her to respond honestly. Once this burden of deceit is lifted, she will be able to get into the spirit of sex wholeheartedly and react with heartfelt abandon. Harry will love her all the more for it.

THE MAGIC TOUCH

Continuous caressing throughout the day usually generates arousal. It can be as simple as stroking a partner's hand at a movie, touching a shoulder briefly in passing, even bodies touching during sleep. But over time, a couple may fall out of the habit of touching each other. They forget how pleasant it feels to touch and be touched.

Getting back into the habit of touching can help bring about a much improved sex life for most couples. Holding hands, giving each other back rubs, running fingertips over a partner's face, all done gently and leisurely, are wonderful ways to begin. This kind of experimentation should take place outside of a sexual context, when both partners are fully clothed and feel no compulsion to "perform." But what can be done when touching between mates is frequent enough, but distasteful for one partner? Take the case of Jennifer, a forty-one year old woman, whose defeated attitude permeated the atmosphere. "I really don't know why I've come," she offered as she entered the office.

"I have been married to Alan for twenty-one years. We have grown children. Our lives together have been pretty well set. How can I expect our love life to change after all of these years?

"Alan spends almost no time alone with me other than at the dinner table. When we are home together, usually on the weekends, and the possibility of sex is probable, he refuses to shave. He works around the house and yard in an old, torn sweatshirt and greasy, baggy, ripped jeans. His baseball cap never leaves his head. I wonder if he will be buried in it.

"When he does approach me, it is usually with a beer in one hand. He will grab me, and give me a smack on the cheek which scratches my face. I hate to say it, but he smells from his exertion in the yard. I want to gasp. Nothing about this is a turn-on. I usually find some excuse to avoid being in the same room with him.

"But sometimes I really need him sexually, and then I find making love with Alan very much less than satisfying. I wish he could understand that when he doesn't shave, and then, when he occasionally does try to kiss me, it hurts. I thought that when the children were grown we would have some private time together. Instead of having a vigorous lover all to myself, I have a man who either ignores me or bruises me. How can I get him to show some romantic interest that is not uncomfortable for me?"

When couples have been together a long time, they sometimes forget how important touching is. Touching is foreplay. Touching is what elevates having sex to making love. When a partner becomes careless and disregards how his touch feels to his mate, then touching becomes an infrequent part of the relationship, and so does sex. This often makes a woman feel cold and undesirable. Even if a woman is able to have an orgasm with little or no touching, she most often feels shortchanged, unloved, and resentful.

Jennifer needed to help Alan see her as a desirable, sexual woman once again. They had been together so many years, he had forgotten she was more than a capable wife and mother. She needed to remind him she was able to satisfy him in more ways than just preparing good dinners. Jennifer needed to tell Alan that when he didn't shave on the weekends and then tried to kiss her, it felt very unpleasant to her. She could tell him how much she appreciated how beautifully he kept their garden and how she depended on his handiness around the house. Expressing her gratitude at seldom having to call on the services of an outside plumber would do a great deal to stroke his ego.

Then, Jennifer could show her appreciation by planning to take a wonderful dinner that Alan obviously enjoyed into the yard on a Saturday evening, perhaps with a bottle of wine. Jennifer could suggest they watch the stars come out while they lay in each other's arms on a blanket and some throw pillows. She might borrow a book from the library, and together try to spot Orion and the Big Dipper. It had been a long time since this couple had done something new together. Just making the plans could bring the spirit of fun and anticipation to Jennifer's attitude, which would naturally spill over into Alan's. Jennifer could prepare strawberries with whipped cream for dessert (overcoming the urge to shave him with the whipping cream) and they could feed the luscious berries to each other. She could put her arms around him and gently stroke those muscles she so admires. When Jennifer learns to please Alan in new and different ways, he will most probably be unable to resist returning the pleasant sensations he is receiving to her.

A subtle way Jennifer could get Alan to shower is by buying him a surprise gift — new cologne and matching soap-on-a-rope. She can tell him this new scent reminds her of him — so cool, strong, and sexy. She can put the rope around his neck and lead him to the shower as she begins to disrobe. She can then enticingly invite him to shower with her, where she can run against him to lather her breasts, back, hands, showing her partner how much all of this turns her on. Then, she can towel dry him and lead him to the bed for a massage. Alan will probably love the response his new fragrance evokes in Jennifer and may not need to be reminded to shower again. They could even make a weekend ritual of a sexy shower together.

When a couple is able to please each other by touch, either while wearing clothing or not, the pressure of performance is alleviated. Paying attention and giving pleasure to each other's bodies is one of the most delightful forms of sexual expression and communication in which a couple can engage. Learning to do what feels wonderful to one another can change a relationship from a sparring match to a love match in which both partners will score.

LOVE MEANS GIVING EACH OTHER PLEASURE

Though touch is very important for partners, it is also very subjective. One person's pleasure may be another person's pain. Stephanie, a thirty-five-year-old aerobics instructor, was unhappy because her husband of three years seemed to have no idea how to touch her.

> "Kurt is always trying to grab me, and I do mean *grab*. He gives me a lot of attention, but it certainly isn't the kind of attention I desire. He is crazy about my long hair, but instead of stroking it gently, he pulls on it, both before and during sex. Sometimes he gets so excited, he actually pulls some of my hair out. When he kisses me, it is with a sucking, wet smack. This is not sexy to me. I feel like I'm being kissed by a mush-mouthed monster. He is always grabbing my thigh and pinching my breasts. I know I am a healthy, athletic woman, but I can't seem to make him realize I am not Wonder Woman. I prefer gentleness, not roughness, during intimacy."

It is always a mystery to a woman that a man does not understand what feels good to her. Certainly if she were to grab his penis and pull hard, he would not find this pleasant. Yet men have difficulty in understanding that rough hands hurt. Enthusiasm is a wonderful attribute in the bedroom, but it is a bedroom — not a jungle. A woman needs to be very tactful when she tells her man that he is hurting her. It is often wiser to show him ways that please her than to simply criticize. When a man has been treating his mate roughly, he has no other frame of reference. She needs to show him how to love her *gently*, but with passion.

Stephanie needs to begin at the top, literally. She loves having her long, lustrous hair admired and stroked, not pulled. She could ask Kurt to wash her hair for her, either in the tub or shower. She could show him how to shampoo her head gently, massaging her scalp, and play with the swirls of delicious-smelling shampoo. When she moans with true pleasure, Kurt will certainly find this a turn-on. She might reciprocate with a wonderful shampoo for Kurt as well. Having one's head gently massaged with aromatic cream is a very sensuous experience. Stephanie might even encourage Kurt to brush her hair, after it is dried, with gentle, lingering strokes. This can be a very erotic shared experience for most couples.

TOUGH LOVE?

Everyone has observed shoppers testing peaches and melons in a supermarket to see if they are ripe. Some shoppers actually squeeze the juice out of a tomato and then reject it for being too ripe. No woman wants to be treated like a piece of produce. Yet, some men pinch and squeeze their partner's breasts and thighs as though they were doing the family shopping, searching for the perfect fruit and vegetables for their enjoyment.

When a woman wants to teach her mate how to treat her, she might try suggesting a bubble bath together. A very romantic atmosphere can be created by placing candles around the tub. No need to worry about having enough candle holders. All she needs to do is melt some wax at the bottom of the candle and adhere it to a saucer. Almost everyone has matching saucers, and the effect created can be most alluring. Then, after disrobing each other in this seductive atmosphere, a woman can ask her mate to wash her with a wash cloth, gently as though she were a baby. There is something about visualizing bathing a baby with a soft cloth and a bar of soap that brings out the tenderness in everyone. She could tell her partner she is completely in his care. Her response to his delicate washing of all parts of her body will be one of complete pleasure. Perhaps she will need

to please him first with his own gentle bath, helping him understand how delicate touching can foster affection, warmth, and ardor.

After bathing, partners may choose to massage each other with
a rich body cream or lotion. If her lover's hands are rough, a woman
could try giving *him* a manicure. This is considered a great luxury
to many men. It will insure no hangnails scraping along her sensitive body, with no complaints about how rough his touch has been.
Another idea is for partners to invite a masseuse into their home to
give a professional massage that will leave each feeling deliciously
sexy toward one another.

When a couple enters into a loving relationship, each partner
trusts the other not to hurt a mate intentionally. But if partners do
not express what feels good to each other verbally, it is impossible
to know what feels pleasant and what does not. Partners need to ask
about each other's preferences during sexual touching. How a mate
answers can greatly affect a sexual relationship. For example, a
woman may love to have her nipples caressed between her partner's
fingertips, but, at certain times of the month, she may be so sensitive that just having her breasts touched at all may be annoying to
her. Partners need to be alert to what causes a positive response, as
well as when that same action causes a negative response.

This is not to say that partners should give constant instruction
during lovemaking. No one likes to be told exactly what to do all of
the time. When a mate demands a partner to go faster or slower or
gives explicit instructions on when and where to rub a body part,
lovemaking becomes a very tedious, unpleasurable procedure.
When partners love, it is important to trust that mates will know
what their preferences are because they have discussed them ahead
of time.

SEXUAL CPR

Occasionally a lover is unfortunate enough to be with a partner who
exhibits almost no physical, emotional, or verbal response in bed,
very much like a dead salmon or, as it is more colloquially referred,
a lox. This may sound amusing, but this situation is definitely not
funny. When two such partners engage in sex, the expectation of an

orgasm is minimal for both. Of course, there are times when a partner is not in the mood for sex, but responding with such statements as "I don't want to have sex now," or "I really don't care how badly you need me, I'm not in the mood" can issue a strong provocation. This partner is saying to a mate, "Try to turn me on, and if I like what you're doing, I may respond." The reasons for such behavior are varied. Perhaps the partner is depressed, or cynical, or using drugs and alcohol. Maybe this person is unsure of his or her own sexual ability or is afraid of displeasing his or her partner. Perhaps a mate does not know how to respond to his or her partner's expressed needs. No matter what the reason, the partner receiving such responses is being hurt. Experts agree, it requires a patient, loving partner to explore what is causing these difficulties.

If a mate decides to invest the time and energy to discover why a partner is behaving in such an aloof and nonemotional manner, the reasons must be impressive. Maybe there has been a long-standing relationship between these two people and these uncaring expressions are unusual and not at all the norm. Perhaps there is a powerful mutual investment, such as children. This couple may have survived great emotional experiences together such as the loss of employment or the death of a parent. Sometimes that partner will be able to succeed in understanding what is bothering his or her mate. When one partner is able to assist the other in expressing feelings in a positive manner, that partner is showing how determined his or her love truly is. Such dedication and resolve can build confidence for both partners. It is true that understanding and forgiveness are the important tools needed to give partners the opportunity to regain love. It is also important to know when the prize is no longer worth the game. Sometimes even the most caring partner needs to admit when he or she cannot break through a partner's protective barriers. In certain situations, it may be wise to say, "Love me, don't hurt me, or I'm history."

I CAN'T TAKE IT ANYMORE!
Lily and Dillan managed to survive years of marriage in spite of the fact that friends and family could not understand what kept them

together. Lily, thirty-one, had married Dillan after a whirlwind courtship. Now, eleven years after the ceremony, Lily sought counseling for her disappointing relationship. Lily's chief complaint was that Dillan was sexually cold toward her and had been for years.

"It is still difficult for me to believe that Dillan is so completely uninterested in sex. I feel fortunate if I can coax him to have sex with me even once a month. I feel frustrated and irritable most of the time. It seems as though I am constantly pleading with him to kiss me or caress me, or even just speak to me nicely. Sometimes I wonder why I stay with him. But how can I leave him when we have two young children who need two parents? No matter how I criticize Dillan's lack of attention to me, he is wonderful with the children.

"When we first met, I was engaged to his best friend, Bob. Bob and I had planned to be married after we had saved enough money to buy a home. I worked as a secretary and Bob was a paralegal who planned to go to law school after we were married. We had been dating for about a year and a half when Bob gave me an engagement ring. It was not a surprise. I picked it out on my lunch hour and Bob made payments on it for months. When he gave it to me, I could hardly wait to call my mother and tell my friends that it had happened at last. Now, they could begin to plan my shower and I could reserve the church. Because we had so little money, Bob and I seldom went out. Most of our evenings were spent at his apartment, planning our future home. On weekends, we would drive from one open house to another getting ideas for what kind of house we would choose when we had enough money. Our relationship was not very exciting. But, it was comfortable. I knew Bob was a hard worker and we had a solid future ahead of us.

"One night we went out to a little Mexican restaurant that wasn't very fancy but had excellent food. The place was packed with couples we knew. My girlfriend, Patsy, came over to the table with the guy she was with and introduced us to him. That man was Dillan. I can't explain the excitement I felt just looking at him. I could feel the blood rushing to my face. I could tell he was immediately taken with me as well. The four of us made polite conversation for a few minutes, and then Bob asked them to join us. I was a nervous wreck. I giggled a lot and my conversation made no sense. Bob blamed my behavior on the beer we were drinking and I accepted his excuses for me. I am not proud of this, but two days later, when Dillan invited me to meet him for a cup of coffee, I accepted. Ours was truly love at first sight.

"Dillan worked in his father's steel company as a salesman. He told me he made his own hours and would like to see me whenever I was able. I made certain he knew that Bob and I were engaged—of course, he could see that I was wearing a ring. But, I did continue to see Dillan while Bob was working or involved with other things. The sexual pull between Dillan and me was so strong, I knew I would have to break it off with Bob. Dillan suggested I write Bob a letter and explain what had happened between us. I wrote a long letter of apology, put it in a box along with my ring, and left it with a note for Bob to find in his mailbox after I had run off with Dillan.

"At first, our marriage was wonderful. Dillan was tender and passionate. We made love almost all the time when we were together. My parents were furious at me for breaking off with Bob the way that I did. My mother said she was ashamed of me. I knew I had to make my marriage work because I could never admit failure to her. Besides, I had nowhere else to go. Dillan's parents could never accept our marriage and my friends wouldn't speak to me. It made no difference to me, then. I was so desperately in love. If my friends and family didn't appreciate my feelings, Dillan and I could get along very nicely without them, or so I thought.

"When I became pregnant with our first child, everything changed. Dillan began coming home later and later. One weekend, he didn't come home at all. I was frantic. We had a terrible fight. We even hit each other with our fists. Not hard. Just because neither of us seemed able to contain our emotions. Then, at the height of the argument, Dillan grabbed me and kissed me long and hard. He told me he was sorry and we ended up in bed making the most passionate love we had ever made before. Dillan said I had provoked his anger by getting pregnant so soon and not allowing him to work as long as he had planned. He told me that when he saw how desperately I needed him, my dependence broke down all his resistance. My neediness turned him on. I was so happy to have the fighting stop and so thrilled with his lovemaking, I was more than willing to forget about the whole thing.

"Unfortunately, that was the beginning of a pattern for Dillan and me. He often seems depressed and we fight constantly. I am in agony with longing for him. Then, we make up in bed and I truly believe the arguing will never happen again. I am certain we are making a new start. I guess I have to make myself feel this way. I can't leave him. Where would I go? How would I take care of my two girls?

THE BAROMETER OF LOVE

Most partners are adept at fooling themselves. Many mates are not in touch with their feelings. But, while it is possible to fool the mind, it is usually impossible to fool the body. Sex is a reflection of the rest of a relationship. When the relationship is not going well, the body does not respond to natural sexual excitement. Sex is the best barometer for telling partners how well a relationship is going and when it is in difficulty. Lily needs to start asking herself some hard questions and giving herself some honest answers.

As painful as it might be for Lily to look realistically at her relationship with Dillan, it could not be more painful than what she is currently experiencing. She needs to chart her answers on paper, so that she can see exactly what is happening and not allow herself to be fooled by what she wishes the answers might be.

She could write something like this:

"When Dillan withholds sex from me and refuses to respond to me sexually, I feel hurt and angry and afraid. The rejection feels very painful to me and I do not want to feel this way any longer. I want to tell Dillan about my feelings. When he tells me that he is not in the mood to make love, and only approaches me after an argument to make up, it makes me feel that I must be doing something wrong, or that he is no longer interested in me."

These words may be difficult for Lily to see in black and white. But, often, when emotions are high, it is impossible for a partner to think clearly. That is why writing thoughts on paper is so valuable. It is possible to correct what is written, but it is impossible to deny the feelings involved in the writing.

When Lily has completed her letter and has taken the time to absorb it, Lily should make a date with Dillan outside the home and away from the children. After a quiet dinner together, she might suggest they go somewhere where they could talk. They might find a little bar with music so that others will not hear what they are saying. Lily could give Dillan her note, expressing her feelings in words that he could read. She needs to remember that Dillan will understand this, because it was he who suggested she tell Bob about her feelings in a letter.

Lily could take Dillan's hands in hers as she gives him the note and tell him how much she really loves him. She could explain that she has difficulty in expressing her feelings verbally, and does not want to have another argument, but it is imperative that Dillan read what she has written. Lily should encourage Dillan to express his feelings as well. Lily could ask Dillan to tell her if he is truly angry with her, or perhaps depressed and would like to have a sympathetic, understanding person to listen to his hopes and fears. She could ask him to express what his expectations are from their marriage, so that she would have a written reminder of Dillan's desires to read during those times when feelings run high and she forgets that they each have deeply felt passions and experienced disappointments.

CHANGE CAN BE THREATENING

It is possible for partners to change sexual feelings of discomfort to sensuous feelings of arousal, but it does take patience. Changing sexual techniques often cause partners to experience feelings they have previously avoided for fear of encountering anxiety, anger, or even guilt. As couples learn to be completely open with one another about their needs and desires, they may feel threatened and try to maintain distance from one another. Couples need to talk about these feelings and express appreciation for each other's real concerns. Changing behavior can be difficult but it is also the route to complete and exhilarating sexual love.

CHAPTER 4

You Want to Do What?

Everyone wonders about his or her own sexual desires and practices. One person's turn-on may be the another person's turn-off. Sometimes a woman may see her mate as perverted when he asks her to engage in certain sexual activities. What is within the bounds of acceptable practices? How can couples establish sexual "comfort zones?"

For decades it was believed there were generally accepted ways of having sex, but they were seldom discussed openly. Sexual myths and misinterpretations were handed down from generation to generation. Today sex is very much an open topic of conversation. Headlines that would make our mothers blush shout out to us from tabloids, books, and magazines. Sometimes partners may feel there is nothing left to be discussed. Therefore, it is puzzling to many couples why there is such a great discrepancy between sexual conversation and what really goes on in the bedroom.

Myths and misunderstandings are what keep couples caught in sexual ruts. Often when a couple experiments with new ways of making love, a greater intimacy develops. Their love lives become more enriched. Sex becomes more exciting. But sexual activity needs to be *mutually* exciting. So, if a woman feels repulsed about any activity her partner suggests, they need to talk about it. Each partner needs to understand what is myth and what is reality, what is arousing and what is repugnant. Compromises need to be reached, so that having sex is mutually rewarding.

When a stunning blonde of thirty named Sally sought advice on sex, it was really quite a surprise. Sally was a local television news reporter any observer would describe as "hip." Dressed in the latest styles and carrying the latest bestseller, Sally proceeded to tell her story.

"For eighteen months now, I have been involved with my fellow anchor on the evening news. It's really no secret—in fact, we are quite a popular couple. We are invited everywhere . . . to charity events, grand balls, and celebrity parties. Jake and I are madly in love and do plan to be married. It's almost perfect except for one thing. Jake wants oral sex. I can neither accept it nor give it. The very idea is repulsive to me. It seems dirty . . . something illicit. Not something a loving partner would want to suggest his mate engage in.

"We have had so many arguments about this. I truly love Jake. How can I handle this situation? Is there something wrong with me, or is Jake asking me to do something unreasonable?"

"This coming Memorial Day weekend Jake and I will be hosting three charity events. We'll be staying in the celebrity suite at the most sumptuous hotel in town. When I told him I was looking forward to getting some rest, he exploded.

" 'Who needs rest? At last. The perfect opportunity to make nonstop love and teach you how to enjoy oral sex. There won't be any interruptions. You won't be distracted by schedules or the sound of the telephone ringing. All you need is a little time and space for me to introduce you to this wonderful way to make love.'

"I was trapped. I literally froze. The thought of performing oral sex was absolutely repugnant to me. Jake might be able to enjoy it, but I cannot imagine becoming so sexually aroused that I would allow him to touch me that way. I'm terrified and I'm dreading the thought of what might happen this weekend."

Jake was not really trying to be insensitive to Sally's wishes. He honestly felt it was his responsibility to introduce her to the magic of oral sex. He believed that once she experienced it, Sally would desire making love in this way as much as he.

It is not unusual for women of an earlier generation to be intimidated by oral sex. Many years ago, sexual mores and sexual knowledge were quite limited. With today's sexually sophisticated couples, reluctance to engage in oral sex is less frequent. In this era of greater sexual freedom, more women are familiar with their bodies and their needs. Many women report experiencing their first sexual orgasm through oral stimulation. Many women do stimulate themselves during masturbation and couples today often find giving each other this kind of pleasure to be sexually satisfying. It was obvious that Sally's concerns stemmed from deeply ingrained beliefs from her childhood.

Sally needs to ask Jake, when they are not engaged in lovemaking, to patiently discuss this issue with her. She needs to make him understand that for her, oral sex feels dirty. Sally could explain how her religious upbringing makes her feel uncomfortable with the idea of oral sex. She could tell Jake she feels shame and repulsion at the very idea of it. Sally needs to be specific. She needs to tell Jake that she does not like the taste or odor and that she finds this an act of perversion. Then, they can discuss ways to reduce the intensity of Sally's feelings, if not to overcome them completely.

Perhaps, with gentle ventures, Jake could assure Sally he would not ejaculate into her mouth. Together they might begin to relax about the subject and approach oral sex as another enjoyable way of sharing an intimate caress. They might discuss the idea that giving and receiving oral sex is only one way of expressing love. Sally could explain to Jake how important it is to her that he never insist she do anything against her will. With time and Jake's patience, Sally might be able to replace her aversion with a new set of attitudes that would bring enjoyment and satisfaction to them both.

BREAKING DOWN MYTHS

If the facts be truly stated, many women enjoy cunnilingus (the correct word for oral sex performed by a man for a woman), and many men are aroused by fellatio (oral sex for a man). There is concern by both men and women that there is a correct way to perform oral sex. One of the major problems for couples in all sexual activity is that they are often obsessed by "the right way." What makes you and your partner feel good *is* the right way.

Don't let yourself become overly concerned with what "everyone else" is or is not doing. Remember, what matters most is *what feels comfortable for you and your partner.*

Brenda's story is another example of partners having difficulties due to their different sexual comfort zones. Donald had asked Brenda to meet him at the airport when he returned from a business trip wearing nothing except her trench coat. Brenda related her shock at her first appointment.

"I really couldn't believe he would ask me to do such a thing. Donald is a consultant who travels the entire country most of the week. We have been married for ten years and have two children, Johnny, eight, and Cindy, five. I am an accountant and work for a large firm here in the city. I am fortunate to have an excellent housekeeper. So, very often, I meet Donald's plane when he returns from a business trip. The airport is just twenty minutes from my office. Usually Donald is tired when he arrives, so we go out for a quick dinner. The children are always in bed by the time we get home. After he checks the mail and the messages, Donald takes a shower and we have a quick sexual encounter in bed. I use the word 'encounter' because there is very little foreplay. It is more like satisfying each other's need than a romantic interlude.

"I have tried to make our love life more exciting. When I do suggest a romantic picnic in the park, Donald questions how we can go without the children. Our vacations are with the children, too, because we both work and feel guilty about spending so little time with them. He doesn't like to buy me presents, because I have very definite tastes and usually purchase what I want for myself. I admit, our life is a little staid, but we go to church on Sundays and take our children to softball and Scouts. Where in the world would he get an idea that I would ever drive through the city nude under my coat? We don't even go to R-rated movies!"

Often when a couple has been together for a long period of time, and one partner suggests something radically different, the other partner feels threatened. She may wonder what gave him such an idea. Has he been with another woman? Why does he want something different from her? Is she an inadequate lover? Is he dissatisfied with her? Is he bored?

Contrary to popular opinion, both men and women are turned-on by erotic situations. Although it is true that men are more aroused by what they see than women, it is also true that both can be visually stimulated. Many women are not used to thinking of themselves as sexual persons. A woman may view herself as a mother and as a professional, but it is sometimes difficult for her to think of herself as an erotic personality. Although this may be an entirely new way of thinking for some women, it can be exciting and fun. It is important to remember, that each of us must take responsibility for his or her own sexuality. One cannot take responsibility for another person. But, if Brenda were able to enter into an erotic adventure, such as meeting Donald at the airport in this sexually explicit way, she might find it as refreshingly stimulating as he.

Brenda and Donald need to share all of their sexual likes and dislikes with each other. Brenda needs to ask Donald what other adventures he would like to share with her. She also needs to tell him what she would like to do. If their activities were planned together, with each partner giving input, then Brenda might feel less intimidated by Donald's unfamiliar request. Brenda, by her own disclosure, would like to have a more interesting sex life with Donald as well. She could suggest they take turns planning erotic rendezvous. She might tell Donald that when she meets him at the airport the next time, she is not taking him to their home. She might reserve a room at a downtown hotel where champagne and hors d'oeuvres await them. There, they might share a leisurely bubble bath and then relax in the sexy lingerie and silk boxer shorts she has brought with her in an overnight bag. Knowing that a trusted baby-sitter is taking care of the children, they could relax and concentrate on getting reacquainted. When they awaken, Donald and Brenda will feel refreshed and ready to give the children a wonderful family weekend together without feeling guilty that they have spent these stolen hours together, alone.

THE THORN IN PORN

It is almost universally accepted that a man is aroused by what he sees, while a woman is aroused by what she feels. When discussing sexual comfort zones, the subject of pornographic videos cannot be overlooked. Once porno movies could only be seen at an X-rated movie house or at a stag party — and these were generally patronized by men. Today porno movies are available at every neighborhood video store, and are viewed at home in privacy. While a man might enjoy a porno movie and feel it really turns him on, his partner is more likely to be repulsed by watching one. This creates another area of controversy for couples. Can viewing pornographic videos be erotically arousing to both men and women? Is it possible to stretch acceptable comfort zones?

Luann, forty and very nervous, gingerly approached the topic that brought her to counseling.

"Stan and I have been together for three years. I met him in my attorney's office, while I was going through my divorce. He handles only tax cases, but my attorney suggested I seek some financial advice from Stan while we were working out my settlement. He is very good looking. Stan had been married before as well. He has a son, seventeen, who lives with his ex-wife in another city. He had been divorced for five years before we met. Stan was very understanding about my problems with my two little girls. His wife had left him, just as my former husband had left us. He understood my feelings of rejection. I was feeling very insecure about myself as a woman. It is not easy when your husband leaves you for a younger, more attractive female. Stan helped restore my confidence. He made me feel very much like a woman again.

"We began dating the very day we met. Stan took me for a cup of coffee across the street from his law offices. We talked so much, I forgot the time. My sitter had to be home by six. Stan offered to drive her. My girls thought he was very funny. He teased them a little and bought them ice cream bars. He said they would have to put them in our freezer until after dinner. They were thrilled with his attention. I was impressed with his thoughtfulness. I asked him to stay and join us, after he dropped off the sitter. Dinner was only frozen pizza and salad, since I didn't have time to cook. Stan took the candlesticks off the dining room table, lit the candles, and put them on our formica table in the kitchen. He poured the girls apple juice and told them to pretend it was wine. "One should always have wine with Italian food,' he teased. We shared an old dusty bottle of red wine I found in the cellar. Stan didn't leave until after midnight. By that time, I knew I wanted to see him again.

"Our relationship blossomed. We liked the same silly movies and taking the girls to amusement parks. Sometimes Stan would take me to a fancy restaurant and then we would go dancing. Most of the time, he would come over for dinner with the three of us. Sometimes he brought take-out. The girls were especially pleased when he brought Chinese food and a video we all would watch together. One evening, after our fourth viewing of *The Little Mermaid* and the children were in bed, Stan proceeded to put another video in the VCR. He told me this was a special treat for me. I was expecting something like *Terms of Endearment,* since he seldom watched a drama and I love a good sob story. Instead, *Bambi Busts Out* appeared on the screen. I was furious. Stan tried to get me to watch a little of it. Everything was so graphic. What would make him think I would like to see all those body parts? The vivacious blonde's breasts were so large, I felt very inadequate. Even though Stan tells me I am attractive, I certainly didn't look like her. The video was very explicit and cheap. Imagine watching a movie like that while my girls were sleeping upstairs? I told Stan I thought I was enough to turn him on. We had a terrible fight. I really love this man and don't want to loose him because of a porno movie."

WHEN WHAT EXCITES HIM FEELS DEGRADING TO HER

Many men feel viewing pornographic videos turns them on. A woman often feels very differently. She questions why a man would want to watch someone else, and then make love to her. She knows she does not look like the person on the screen. Watching someone with huge breasts and no noticeable imperfections can make any woman more aware of what she feels are her inadequacies.

There is almost no woman alive who is satisfied with her own body. She wishes her breasts were larger or smaller. She is usually always watching her weight. She would give up chocolate forever, if it would make the cellulite disappear. Most men never see these imperfections. Or, if they do, it doesn't matter. A man loves a woman for her *response to him.* If men only fell in love with women who looked like Raquel Welch, very few women would be in relationships.

Many men like to see other couples making love. The visual impact arouses most men. Until very recently, makers of X-rated films seemed to produce them for men only. They were insensitive to a woman's more aesthetic tastes. Now there are porno movies made by women. The couples acting in them are often married to each other. The partners look more like real people. The situations acted out are more usual and the settings are less exotic. Many women find they can watch these movies with their partner because they can relate to the man and woman on the screen. They do not feel in competition with the actress, but relate to her much as they do to their favorite female movie star. These movies can be very helpful to couples. They present new and exciting techniques for making love without portraying grossly sexual situations.

Luann needs to tell Stan that she is in love with him and hopes he loves her, too. She needs to explain that in her upbringing the viewing of pornographic movies was considered taboo. It is very important for her not to put down his tastes, but to make it clear these feelings come from her childhood. Many women are taught by their mothers and society that "nice girls just don't do that kind of thing." These lessons were appropriate to protect her when she was young. That somehow gets translated into the bedroom years after a woman has become an adult.

Luann needs to make Stan understand that she feels these movies are degrading to women. A woman may feel that when her man wants to watch someone else making love, he is not making love to her. Luann wanted sex with Stan to be less explicit and more refined. It is important for her to make it clear that she is interested in exploring new sexual techniques. Perhaps they could rent one of the newer videos produced by a woman. She might even try to view a movie of Stan's choice for a few minutes. Often it is the unfamiliarity of a new experience that frightens and turns a woman off. If Stan could be patient with Luann, in time she might accept this form of sexual stimulation as fun and exciting. If she doesn't, though, maybe they could come up with something they both feel comfortable with.

Sex is the ultimate way for couples to show love and desire. When a lover makes sexual overtures to a mate, that partner is asking for acceptance. When a partner denies sex, for whatever reason, a mate may feel rejected and unloved. Sometimes mates take these hurtful feelings to someone else's bed. That is why it is important to remember that if a partner does not want to have sex with a mate at a particular time, it should be made clear that it is the *sex* that is not wanted. Not the mate. Partners need to constantly reinforce loving feelings for each other.

SEXUAL COMFORT ZONES MUST BE MUTUALLY DETERMINED

Couples need to discuss openly what does and does not feel comfortable to them. Often a partner will suggest something that is completely foreign to his mate. Her initial response might be the same as the first time she tried calamari. She might gag and refuse to sample what is offered. Then, after a small taste, she might decide this is an excellent food to order on special occasions, but not as a part of a steady diet.

A woman is much more likely to be receptive to new techniques for pushing beyond present sexual comfort zones when she is a part of the decision-making. It takes patience and understanding from both partners. A woman should be careful not to ridicule her partner's suggestions in any way because he will probably become defensive. She should discuss what bothers her about his request. Then, the couple should try to find a different way to approach it. A woman may find one suggestion totally unacceptable to her. But, if she is willing to offer a compromise, her partner will respect her and she will respect herself. Finding sexually exciting turn-ons is all part of the adventure.

For sex to be a success, both partners must be comfortable. One partner should never try to force another to engage in something that partner feels is embarrassing or upsetting. If every partner's needs were constantly being satisfied, there would be no need to explore or experiment with new ideas or ways of relating to one another. It is only when partners feel boredom, frustration, or pain that they seek other means of satisfaction.

In successful relationships, couples realize this is an ongoing process. Almost always thoughtful loving requires negotiation between the partners. There is no one right way to make love. What may seem inappropriate or frightening or even abhorrent to a mate at one period of time, might seem titillating at another. The secret, if there is just one secret, is to keep reinvesting in the relationship. If you care enough, give your very best, but only if and when it feels right to you. There are many ways to participate in exciting sex. A couple only needs to find what works for them.

WHEN LOVE HURTS

There are times when a woman may experience pain while making love. It is important for every woman to know that sex does not have to hurt. When a woman does experience discomfort, and even pain, when making love, the reason is most often physical, not psychological. It is rare that a woman will experience emotional conflicts so intense that her feelings of sexual excitement are completely diminished. In extreme situations, such as rape or incest, or other physical or emotional trauma, all sexual feeling might cease until there is a psychological resolution of the problem. If a woman does experience pain when she's touched or feels so ticklish that she is unable to relax her body, she should seek professional help immediately. A specialist who deals with deep emotional stress is readily available by calling a family physician or a local hospital.

Coital discomfort, or pain during sex, is a common complaint that almost every woman experiences at some time in her life. This situation may occur after childbirth, when a woman is breast-feeding her baby, or during the menstrual cycle. A woman may also experience dryness a few days before or after her period. One of the most frequent times women report sexual *indifference* and *discomfort* is following menopause. Unfortunately, often a woman will hesitate to consult a physician about the problem because she does not realize there is usually relief for coital discomfort or pain. She may be too embarrassed or uncomfortable to discuss these changes in her sex life with either her doctor or a competent therapist because she mistakenly believes it is only happening to her. Every woman needs to know that help is available. Sex does not have to hurt.

Evelyn and David had recently celebrated their thirty-fourth wedding anniversary when Evelyn entered sex therapy. An accomplished artist of some renown, Evelyn expressed irritation during her session at her greatly diminished interest in sex.

"David is really the reason I have sought counseling. He thinks there is something very wrong with me, and, he may be right. In our thirty-four years of marriage, we have enjoyed an active sex life. I attribute much of it to our mutual interest in everything around us. We both have a great deal of energy and zest for living. I believe that has been reflected in our sex life, until recently. David is a surgeon who reads every mystery novel available when he isn't seeing one of his patients. His hobbies are varied. He plays tennis four times a week and likes to collect old books in his spare time. He is always on the phone with dealers throughout the country. On trips, we spend hours exploring old dusty bookstores. Once he found a first edition which he sold to a dealer for one hundred dollars. He discovered later it was worth much more. David said that for him the thrill of the discovery could not be valued in terms of money. He is in excellent physical condition and still turns heads with his sculptured features, stark white hair, and terrific physique.

"As you now, I have enjoyed limited fame as a watercolorist. My paintings still win prizes and I am constantly being asked to enter shows throughout the country. I love my profession. When I first began painting, as a young girl, I thought I would never marry. I planned to travel the world and live a Bohemian lifestyle. Then, I broke my leg skiing and needed to consult an orthopedic surgeon. David recognized both my name and my work when I saw him in consultation. We began dating after my recovery and have spent all these many good years together. I do travel, sometimes alone. We decided not to have children, so that I could devote myself entirely to David and my painting. My professional life as well as my personal has seemed very fulfilled.

"I experienced minimal discomfort during menopause. I suffered a few lower back pains and some headaches, but, for the most part, nothing seemed to bother me very much. I viewed menopause with a feeling of relief. It was a pleasure not to have the monthly inconvenience of my periods. What is bothering me, though, is the steady waning of my sex drive. During the past few months, whenever David approaches me, I plead off. When he begins to penetrate me vaginally, it hurts. I don't know whether it hurts because I am not having sex as much as I used to or that I am not having sex as much as I used to because it hurts. I only know that both David and I are unhappy about the situation. Is there any help for me?"

Evelyn's situation is not unique. Many women experience problems with sex after menopause. Lack of sexual interest very often does result in sexual aversion. When a woman feels dryness and penetration is painful, it is natural for her to avoid making love. It is certainly not pleasant to have sex when it hurts. Every woman with this problem needs to differentiate when and where the pain does occur. To do this accurately, she needs the help of a doctor.

A physician will be able to determine if the physical pain is occurring inside or outside a woman's vagina. A physician may be able to locate an infection and treat it effectively. It is important to have a thorough physical examination of the entire genital tract to rule out organic disorders and anomalies. A physician will help a woman ascertain the time and the site of pain, which is imperative to determine both the cause and the solution. Approaching the problem from a physical perspective helps diffuse the emotional aspect of the situation. Professional reassurance can help a woman better deal with the fears and anxieties this kind of situation can bring on.

Evelyn may be suffering from a distinct lack of lubrication, which is common to post-menopausal women. Penetration is much easier when the wall of the vagina responds to "sexy feelings" by giving off a liquid that lubricates the entrance to the vagina. As a woman ages, this lubrication needs to be enhanced. There are numerous excellent products on the market that a gynecologist can recommend. Years ago, some of these products were sold only in sex shops, but today, in our more enlightened society, they are available in almost every pharmacy. Evelyn should ask her doctor which product is best for her.

When a woman is concerned about having sex, the entrance to her vagina may tighten. Inserting the penis may be very painful. Experts stress timing is all important. If a partner tries to insert the penis before the woman is fully aroused, she still might be too tight, even though she is wet enough. Partners should not rush. A woman needs to ask her mate to take his time and be patient with her. As a man ages, he is often concerned with losing his erection and tries to penetrate the woman as quickly as possible, while he is still able. A woman needs to explain lovingly and carefully, that rushing sex, no matter what the age or reason, will seldom have positive results. Whatever is causing the pain, no one needs to live with it. When sex is uncomfortable, a woman needs to find out why. Until she does, she needs to find other ways of making love. It is the right and the responsibility of every woman to discover what will make her life more satisfying. Evelyn and all women need to exercise that power.

MORE THAN A SLIGHT IRRITATION

Kristy was forty-one when she found herself divorced and in need of a job. Her two children were in college and the new apartment was lonely. Besides, she could never survive on the alimony she would be receiving from her ex-husband. Kristy had not worked since Kevin, her oldest son, was born. When reviewing her job skills, Kristy realized she had very few. Her typing ability was minimal. Besides, today everyone requires computer knowledge. Computers were a complete mystery to Kristy, one which she had no desire to solve. Two Sundays in a row she scanned the classifieds. Nothing seemed appealing. Then, on one Saturday evening, she was at a dinner party given by one of her few remaining friends, when one of the guests suggested she apply as receptionist at the office of one of the city officials. Kristy knew almost everyone in the town from her past volunteer experience. Her personality was outgoing and dynamic. The guest who suggested the idea, one of her friend's husbands, was certain he could pull some strings to get her the job.

When Kristy first sought counseling, this is what she shared.

"Boy, could he pull strings. My friend's husband did help get me the job. But, the strings he wanted to pull were mine. I was grateful, but, not *that* grateful. After I got the job, I called Mr. X to thank him for all his considerable help. He suggested meeting to celebrate with drinks later. I met him, and got completely bombed on two martinis on an empty stomach. He offered me a lift to my car, instead of the ride home that I really needed. It turned out to be a struggle. I thought I'd never escape his groping hands. I guess he thought I would be lonely, which I was, and horny, which I also was. I just wasn't interested in making out with my friend's husband in the front seat of his car, or anywhere else. She never did understand why I declined all her future invitations to dinner. Especially after her husband had been so "kind." How could I tell her? But, the real problem for me was not my lack of dinner invitations. I found, after that miserable first experience of being single again, that I was unable to enjoy sex. I could not come to orgasm.

"My new boss was single and very good looking. He had silver wavy hair and a gorgeous smile. I could see why he had been repeatedly elected to public office. The work, though challenging for me in the beginning, was really very easy. I took his numerous messages, for he was seldom in the office, made appointments for him, and kept the coffee pot going. I had the opportunity to dress very nicely for this position where I was constantly in touch with the public. I really loved my job. After I had been working for Don for about two weeks, he invited me to attend a fund-raising dinner as his guest. We made a very attractive couple. As we were both so well-known in the community, people immediately assumed we were going together. I did nothing to dispel these observations. Let my ex-husband hear about it. Make him a bit jealous for a change.

"That first fund-raiser was the start of a serious relationship for us. Our interests were much the same. He was kind and considerate and took me to wonderful places. My life seemed to be happy again. Then, we went to bed. As patient and thoughtful as Don tried to be with me, all I could think about was the comparison between Don's way of making love and that of my ex, Garth. Garth had been a fantastic lover. Of course, he got lots of practice. With other women, that is. Now, when I finally got the opportunity to have sex with someone who wanted to be exclusively with me, I was unable to come to orgasm. Sex hurt. Why? It doesn't seem fair."

Many women enter therapy after a divorce in order to separate sexual feelings with a new partner from those in a former relationship. These unresolved feelings often manifest themselves in the bedroom. Having sex with a new partner after the dissolution of an old relationship can be traumatic for both men and women. Of course, these problems need to be addressed psychologically. There are some things partners can do when sex hurts during a new relationship.

Kristy needs to know that these problems are not exclusively hers. Especially in today's world, so many fears involving sex are brought to a new relationship. The main concern of all couples is sexually transmitted disease. People die of AIDS. This presents a serious aspect to serendipitous sex. It is amazing that some partners do not take this threat seriously. Some couples still view the prospect of contracting AIDS as something that happens to someone else, like a car accident. Partners presume if a mate has contracted herpes, that prospective lover will say so up front, and allow his potential partner to decide if he or she will have protected sex or decline the offer entirely.

No matter how wonderful and caring a prospective partner may seem, no one knows who a potential mate has previously been with. Therefore, Rule Number One! It is imperative to use a condom. It is sexually correct for a woman to carry condoms today. Just as women have always been the sex concerned most about birth control, it is not at all surprising that women have taken the initiative in protecting themselves. For those who may not be aware, condoms now are available in attractive carrying cases. This is important information for women concerned about what people will think if her purse spills and the contents are viewed by her mother or a great aunt. Condoms are also available in numerous flavors. Perhaps one should carry a variety. A potential lover might prefer strawberry to licorice. Levity aside, be adult about condoms. Teenagers unfortunately often don't use protection because they are afraid of spoiling the mood or they feel guilty about appearing as though they were expecting to have sex. Adults take care of themselves. When couples have been planning every way possible to be able to engage in sex, it does seem ridiculous to pretend it is the last thing on a partner's mind. Although both partners might be unsure of who is to bring the condoms, mates can suggest that one bring the condoms and the other bring the wine.

In a new and unfamiliar relationship, sex might hurt a woman because her partner is unsure of when she is sufficiently lubricated. Just because she is wet does not mean a woman is ready for penetration. Pain can be decreased or eliminated when partners assume new and different positions. Sometimes sex hurts because a woman may be reacting to the vaginal irritation caused by a birth control foam, cream, or jelly. Some women react to the rubber in a condom or a diaphragm. Vaginal deodorant sprays have been known to irritate the vagina or the vulva. The reasons and the occasions for sex to hurt are as numerous as the couples involved.

It is important for a woman to be able to discuss this problem with someone she feels is listening and really cares about what she is saying. When a woman does consult a professional, and she feels her needs are not being met, she should feel free to consult another authority. It is a partner's prerogative to question any aspect about sex.

CHAPTER 5

What Worked on Tuesday May Not Work on Wednesday

Most couples get into sexual ruts at one time or another during the course of a relationship. Sometimes sex can feel exactly like a AAA trip ticket to Ashtabula; you know the route is the same every time. Most couples find the most enjoyable sex is the most comfortable sex. When couples limit themselves to these tried and true routines, sexual boredom can result. This can and usually does have a negative effect on sexual desire.

Partners who are able to talk freely about sex will probably find it easier to tackle problems like this. Let's face it. It is not always easy to talk about sexual matters. But, sex does matter — very much. So, couples need to remember that good lovers are made, not born. There are steps that couples can take to provide sexual variety in their lovemaking style. If partners can act on these varying approaches and trust each other enough not to be afraid to improvise, rejuvenating an uninspired sex life can be a lot of fun.

"For years now, Saturday evening has been the one night of the week I can plan that Cal will want to have sex." This information was grudgingly offered by Trina, a thirty-nine-year-old fashion consultant seeking relief from what she found to be a boring marriage. "If I suggest we make love on Wednesday night or Thursday morning, God forbid, Cal's reaction is explosive. I wish our sex life were.

"Everyone thinks that because I work as a fashion consultant, my life is very glamorous. Well, it's not. Women in their sixties wearing size two dresses are about the only people who can afford my services, and there aren't too many of them. Dresses and sportswear that belong on a much younger person are carted off by customers I have convinced look just marvelous in them. I used to think if I had access to an unlimited wardrobe, my life would be perfect. My mood could be brightened by every change of clothing. My personality would broaden with every different costume. One outfit would reflect my daring side, another, my mysterious but lovable nature. Not so. Dealing with hypersensitive models and colors almost no one can wear can be very tedious. Sometimes I feel so irritable, it is a wonder Cal wants to make love to me at all. It has taken me years to get this job. I wouldn't trade it for another, but I do want some excitement and variety in my personal life.

"Although we have been married for only eight years, Cal and I have been together for twelve. We met in college. He was a track star and I was studying marketing and fashion design. Cal is a computer programmer. I must confess, sometimes I feel as though he were programming me when he begins to make love to me. It is always the same. Never a variation. I can tell when he clears his throat in a certain way while we are watching television exactly what he has in mind for later, after the eleven o'clock news. Never before. If I do suggest something new, something I've read in a magazine, he tells me that I am being silly. Cal says real people don't do those things. He feels those articles are written just to sell magazines. I have tried buying sexy lingerie. Cal seldom notices. I didn't even get a positive response when I greeted him at the door last week in pink hot pants and cowboy boots. My exasperation is so close to the surface that no matter what Cal says, I snap at him. What happened to the man I thought was so exciting? How can I get some zest back into this marriage? It's not that I don't love him, it's just that I'm bored doing things in the same old way.

"When Cal and I were first together, I found his slightest touch gave me goose bumps. Just watching him undress would turn me on. He would unbutton his shirt so slowly it was maddening. I usually would try to help him. Cal never seemed to mind. In fact, I think he enjoyed my impatience. He really does have a great body. He works out at a health club three times a week and jogs every morning before he leaves for work. Even after all these years, he is just as trim as when we first met. In the beginning, we did try several different positions . Cal bought a book at the campus bookstore. It was fun to experiment. Sometimes we would get so tangled in each other's arms and legs when we tried a new position we would get the giggles and end up just hugging each other. Having orgasms was not our final goal back then. We knew there would always be a next time. We were just happy to be together. After a while, we settled into one or two ways of having intercourse because they were the most comfortable. I was able to reach orgasm almost every time. Cal is not a flamboyant man. He is steady and quiet. I really don't expect him to swing from the chandelier. But, I would like a little variety. I crave a little adventure in my life."

VARIETY: THE SPICE OF LIFE

Couples usually practice sex in a way that feels most comfortable to them. It is often difficult for a partner to want to experiment when the way the couple usually has sex feels so good. When one partner feels bored with the same routine, it is not helpful to criticize and complain. All this does is make the other partner feel angry and inadequate. Then, avoidance sets in. "Not tonight, honey. I feel tired and am going to turn in early," replaces even boring sex. No one wants that to happen. But what is a couple to do?

Trina needs to reassure Cal that she is still very much in love with him. She needs to reinforce the positive feelings she feels toward him. She could tell him how pleased she is that he had stayed so physically attractive and how much she appreciates that he is just as firm and muscular as the day they married. As hard as she has tried to gain Cal's attention, she is not succeeding. Trina needs to attract Cal's attention in a way he will appreciate. She could become more caring and playful toward him without saying one critical thing about his lovemaking. The ways in which she could show how much she cares are as limitless as her imagination.

When a partner wishes to evoke a different sexual response from her mate, that partner needs to behave differently. Trina might try to be more loving toward Cal outside the bedroom. She could touch him in intimate areas of his body when she feels no one is looking or when they are alone. It can be sexually stimulating to touch a partner when there is a risk of being seen — the unexpected can be a real turn-on. Call will not help but feel more intrigued by her surprising behavior. Trina might run her fingers through his hair and put her arms around him when they are sitting together on the couch reading or watching television. She might read aloud some of the steamiest portions of a sexy novel while she runs a bath for Cal.

Trina needs to feel free to initiate as well as to refuse a sexual encounter. If she feels all the responsibility for the couple's sexual success is being placed on her, she should remember that these same suggestions could apply to her partner as well. *It is the partner who is the most aware who can effect the changes in a marriage.* It is impossible to make Cal do what Trina wants him to do. She can only change herself. But, when she does, Cal's response to her will most certainly change as well.

IMAGINATION IS THE GREATEST SEXUAL ASSET

When sex becomes a little stale, a woman could consider this a challenge to her imagination. Sex does not begin in the bedroom. It begins in the mind. All the techniques in the world will seem forced and ineffective if the feelings between the partners are not there to begin with. A man needs to be sensitive to a woman's mood swings that occur with her menstrual cycle. A woman needs to make him feel loved and wanted even when he is not behaving in a particularly loving way. Couples need to be aware of each other's insecurities. They need to talk about what their needs are. This continuous discussion about sexual desires can become a game. Constant conversation about what will make each partner happy will keep a marriage from becoming stagnant. The requests can be as wild as pretending to be strangers meeting each other for the first time in a bar and going home together or as serious as a woman wanting her partner to listen to her when she is unhappy and then taking her in his arms, wiping away the tears, and making passionate love to her. The important thing is to be sensitive to each other's needs. In order to be responsive, couples need to fully understand what those needs are.

WHEN YOU DON'T UNDERSTAND *YOU*

Anger can be a real culprit to love. It can sometimes erupt at the most unexpected times. Because most partners are afraid of expressing negative feelings, they will often try to bury these unpleasant emotions. Then, what a surprise when they seem to explode at a very inopportune moment, such as during lovemaking. Sex can be a way of expressing all kinds of feelings, not just lust, but grief and joy and disappointment. Couples need to define sexual expression both for themselves and for each other. All mates need to understand that everyone has moods. What might seem fine and under control one day might feel quite different on another. Expressing feelings is what sex is all about.

Marilyn, a polished-looking woman in her forties, was completely puzzled by her own behavior. She and her husband, Brian, had a good relationship for the most part.

"Sure, the kids drive me crazy and my mother-in-law gets on my nerves. She is always suggesting better ways to discipline the boys and more efficient ways to clean my house. We do argue occasionally about my job. She doesn't approve. I sell real estate, and that requires a lot of time away from my family on evenings and weekends. My mother-in-law feels my children are too young for me to be working away from our home. But they are busy with school and homework and their own activities. I make good money from my sales and we can certainly use it. It gets me out of the house. After all, why should I be the only one at home during the day?

"Although we have been married for seventeen years, Brian's and my sex life is usually very pleasant. When I've had it up to here, we go away for a weekend. Usually we go to a bed and breakfast. The pace is low-key. It gives us time away from the responsibilities of the children and our jobs so that we can talk and spend some loving time together.

"Until recently, almost everything Brian did in bed pleased me. Lately I find I am impatient with his touch. If he kisses me, I find it too rough. When he reaches for me in bed, I want him to be more tender. I am having trouble coming to orgasm. I try not to say anything, but it is difficult to ignore my feelings. Why am I feeling this way?"

Most women are taught to please from early childhood. Almost all mothers teach their daughters to be good little girls. In sexual relationships, women also try to please their mates. When a woman feels angry toward her mate, those unresolved feelings often result in withholding sex from her partner. From what Marilyn described in her session, she was annoyed that her husband had not supported her more fully in the ongoing interference of her mother-in-law. Marilyn felt she was a good mother and wife who contributed to the support of the family by her hard work. She wanted her husband to prevent his mother's criticism, or at least to support Marilyn more actively. Because this had not happened, Marilyn was having trouble enjoying sex.

Couples need to learn how to disagree without destroying their relationship. Most partners never learn how to deal with anger and resentment in an effective manner. A man's and a woman's way of dealing with negative emotions is usually very different. If a woman is upset or angry, her emotions are almost always reflected in the bedroom. A man is able to argue with his wife quite bitterly and then want to have sex with her immediately after the disagreement. A woman is usually not able to do so, because she is now somewhat emotionally detached.

In order for Marilyn to convince Brian of her need for support when his mother interferes, Marilyn needs to speak up. She should not bring up the subject when she is feeling resentful or angry. Marilyn needs to take the time to sort out her thoughts and to clarify her position. She needs to determine what the real issue is and what she wishes to accomplish. Marilyn needs to tell Brian that lately she has been feeling tense and irritated. She needs to tell him that, even though it might be unreasonable, she is disturbed because of his mother's criticisms about how she manages their home and their children. It is important that Marilyn not blame Brian's mother. She needs to take responsibility for her own feelings. She could tell him she wishes the remarks did not bother her so much, but they do. She needs to ask Brian to help her with those feelings of resentment, because they are carrying over into their bedroom.

No one partner is responsible for a mate's sexuality. That duty is impossible for any partner to assume. In a sexual relationship, both partners give and receive pleasure. It is helpful to keep in mind how a woman's response can change from one time to another. What feels wonderfully thrilling to her on one day may be irritating or painful on another. Therefore, it is extremely important for Marilyn to communicate with Brian just what her current sexual mood is. This does not always have to be done verbally. For example, if Brian touches her breasts in a way that feels annoying to her, she can take his hand and guide it to the area of her body she would like him to touch. Then she can tell him how good that feels. Learning to communicate so that both partners learn and respond to each other's desires makes it possible for each sexual experience to be spontaneous. In this way, they are less likely to fall into a routine or a sexual trap.

A partner cannot be expected to be a mind reader. No one can constantly be looking for signs of what the other wants or is feeling. A mate who feels responsible for her partner's sexuality sees that sexual responsiveness as a reflection on him- or herself. This is unrealistic. Giving and receiving pleasure means the physical and emotional involvement of both partners. But, each must share the responsibility for making his or her sexual encounters as rewarding as possible. Sharing this responsibility means communicating and trusting. Trust allows both partners the freedom to focus on individual pleasure.

WHOSE SEXUAL FANTASY?

With so much sexually explicit material bombarding our daily lives, it is not at all surprising that a certain degree of dissatisfaction might occur in the sex life of any couple. Movies depict sexual encounters in ways that many might have never imagined. It is difficult not to compare Michael Douglas's on-screen energetic performance with that of one's own partner. Magazines that once featured such burning topics as fashionable skirt lengths now tell couples how to experiment with kinky sex. Although many find these suggestions embarrassing, there are couples who do wish to experiment. But experimentation needs to be a shared desire. Because partners like something different today, does not mean they will want to do it tomorrow.

When Carla and Mike arrived for counseling, they had been married for three years. Mike, a successful architect, and Carla, a corporate attorney, were very much in love. During her first appointment, Carla spoke of a particularly embarrassing position in which Mike put her.

"I work long hours. I am trying to become a partner in an all-male law firm. You can imagine what dedication that takes. Mike has been supportive, for the most part. He seldom complains when I am too tired to cook. We have help with the cleaning. He understands I do not want to plan a family for a few years yet. I am still in my twenties, so I'm not concerned about my biological clock.

"Last Sunday was a bridal shower for my niece, Tammy, who is just graduating from college. There were the usual linens and bath towels and a few very pretty night gowns. Since I have been so busy, Mike purchased the gift for Tammy. I was shocked when she opened the package. Inside was a black merry widow, a black lace garter belt, stockings with seams, some high-heeled pumps with pom poms, and a small bottle of expensive perfume. The card, which Tammy read out loud, said, 'Here's to keeping your marriage HOT.' How degrading! I turned beet red, gave Mike a glaring look, and just wanted to die. My family thought it was a riot. They laughed and congratulated Mike on his original selection. I have been angry with him since Sunday. Certainly he knows how I feel about a woman being treated as a sexual object. How could he reduce Tammy, me, and all women to this level?"

Mike, quite obviously, was giving Tammy the present he wanted to give himself. He wanted Carla to behave more sensuously when they were alone. He wanted her to be more playful in their lovemaking. Although it is true that Mike accepted Carla as an equal, he wanted her to be his erotic partner in the bedroom. Perhaps his judgment was not the best, but Mike was clearly stating his own sexual fantasy by giving Tammy the slinky, lusty engagement present.

Carla needs to discuss with Mike what he would like to do in bed. If he feels their sex life needs a little spice, even a little fantasy, they could decide together what that might be. If Carla feels uncomfortable with dressing erotically, she might decide to try it once to please him. Mike, in turn, would need to fulfill Carla's sexual desires. She might find it exciting for Mike to fill their tub with strawberry Jell-O (planned, of course, for a day before their house-keeper came). Some women feel that cleanliness aids their sexual arousal. In this spirit, Carla might ask Mike to join her in the shower or in their jacuzzi. Many men find a partially dressed woman more enticing than one who is completely nude. Carla might surprise Mike when he returns from the corner to buy a newspaper by greeting him at the door in a bikini, without the top.

It is necessary for this couple to discuss how important it is for neither of them to embarrass the other in public. When one partner has strong feelings about sex, it is a personal matter Problems in the boudoir are not to be shared with the outside world. But, having a sense of humor is a delightful form of sexual enticement, as long as that humor is not used to make a partner feel uncomfortable.

HIGH EXPECTATIONS

Current books and magazine articles tell women what to expect from their lovers. Is it truly surprising, then, if a woman's expectations are high? If a couple's life does not include such sensual intrigue, partners can feel shortchanged. Moreover, a woman can feel something is wrong with her partner or with herself if their sex life is less than explosive.

Even though a woman requests her partner touch her in a certain way, that touch may feel mechanical to her if she is not feeling lovingly receptive toward her mate. Giving orders usually defeats the purpose of sex. During intercourse, each partner is completely vulnerable. Most couples want sex to be the unguarded release of intense emotions. A man and a woman desire the feeling of oneness with their lover. It is impossible to feel this completeness if a partner is placed in the position of being the director. An imaginative partner can do a lot to change sexual boredom into stimulating pleasure without one command.

"Fred is the most caring man in the world," Cindy reported during her first session. "He brings the children their favorite books and takes the boys to the movies on Saturdays. He pays all the bills on time and cuts the grass every week. I lack for nothing I really need. It is just that he is so boring." Cindy went on to describe her relationship with Fred.

"I met Fred at a school dance when he was home on leave from the service. He looked so handsome in his uniform. He knew he was being sent to Germany soon and was very concerned about living in a foreign country. He asked me to write to him and I did. When he returned from the service, I was working at the local hardware store in my small home town. Nothing very exciting had ever happened to me and I didn't think it ever would. Fred asked me to come to the city with him when he landed a job at the Ford plant. He thought that we could get to know each other better much faster if we were living in the same place. Besides, it was too expensive for him to come to see me at home on weekends. My parents were scandalized. I'm from a very religious family. My dad told Fred if he wanted me to come to the city to live, he'd better declare his intentions real quick. Fred asked me to marry him. I did. That was thirteen years ago.

"I had no previous sexual experience before I married Fred. He was patient with me and I appreciated that. Living in a city was exciting for me. I loved our little apartment. We fixed it up together, mostly with furniture from the Salvation Army or pieces Fred made in his basement tool shop. He has really become a very good woodworker. He enjoys making things with his hands. Fred liked his job and got regular raises. Soon we bought our house and the three children came. Except for wishing Fred were more exciting in bed, I really have no complaints. We do not make love very often anymore. When he comes near me, everything Fred tries to do annoys me. And yet, I long for his sexual attention. Does it seem unreasonable to want more of a sex life after all these years, even though I act unhappy about it when Fred suggests we make love? I am so tired of faking my satisfaction. I want to feel the real thing."

What Cindy was not saying, and perhaps did not recognize, was that Fred was boring, not only in bed. She found it difficult to be excited by him even when they were not making love. Fred's interests were solitary. This couple engaged in almost no mutual activities. Cindy needs to encourage Fred to participate in something they might share so that she could view him in a different light.

When couples have problems with perception, it is always a good idea for them to find something they enjoy doing together. Cindy could suggest to Fred that they take dancing lessons at their local community center. The classes are inexpensive and would enable them to meet new people and expand their social life. Cindy might enjoy planning with the other women what they would wear and where they would go for refreshments after the lessons. Dancing would give both Cindy and Fred something to look forward to. The physical contact of being held while listening to romantic music would help to create an intimate atmosphere which could carry over into their bedroom.

ACTION STIMULATES THE HEART AND OTHER PARTS

Cindy had mentioned Fred's love of woodworking. She could share with Fred how sensuous she felt just thinking about the gentle way in which he fashioned what he was making. She could tell him how exciting she found the way he touched the wood. She might suggest that Fred translate that subtle touch to her body. By taking his hand in hers, she could show him how she wished to be stroked. While lying close together in bed, Cindy could demonstrate to Fred how she would like to have him massage her back and neck and stomach. He might tentatively touch and kiss her breasts and inner thighs, all while she was telling him how delightful his touch felt to her. These actions would certainly generate some excitement in their sex life.

The process of exploring each other's bodies could gradually lead to intercourse. The exhilaration and expectation each of them brings from the dance floor could effectively be translated into a more spontaneous love life for both Cindy and Fred.

PLAY IT AGAIN, SAM

"If Larry sings that song to me one more time, I think I'll scream," confided Sandi after several sessions of getting nowhere with her dwindling relationship. Sandi and Larry met at a club where he was the featured singer and she was the manager. When Sandi first heard Larry perform, five years earlier, she described her initial response as feeling like she was melting.

"He could really sell a song, and he certainly sold me. I was used to listening to male vocalists. Several of them had performed at the club during the years I had been the manager. I always kept my distance, no matter how attractive they were. The last thing I needed was to fall for some guy who had every woman in the club drooling over him. I didn't need that kind of an egocentric relationship. Besides, entertainers are always looking to make it big and move on. Who needs a life on the road? So, I listened, but I ignored Larry's attempts to involve me in any kind of conversation when his sets were over.

"Night after night, this little blond with big hair came to listen to Larry sing. Usually she was with a crowd of kids who looked to be about college age. Then, she began coming into the club all by herself in time for the last set. It was obvious to me she wanted Larry to notice her and take her home. Some little rich brat trying to make it with the talent. We didn't need that kind of trouble in our club. I was trying to figure out how to handle the situation after it had been going on for about two weeks, when one night she comes in with a man old enough to be her father. I walked over to check out the picture a little further when I overheard the conversation. Maybe the man was a record mogul and Little Miss Perfect had brought him to listen to Larry sing hoping her daddy would offer him a contract. That did it! I had been around this business for years. If this was happening in my club, I wanted to be a part of the action.

"Between sets, I cornered Larry at the bar. He seemed delighted that I was finally paying some attention to him. I told him what the scoop was. Larry dismissed my news with a wave of his hand and escorted me over to the table to meet his brother-in-law and his niece, Georgia. At first I was terribly embarrassed. But Larry and his brother-in-law, Dick, thanked me for having treated all the young people who had come to the club with such respect. 'It isn't easy for them to find a place to listen to real music. Most clubs play rock and rap and cater to a different type of crowd. At least there are some members of the younger generation who still enjoy the old standards and you and this club make it possible for them to hear them.'

"After my initial embarrassment, Larry and I began to talk regularly. I guess you could say we became friends before we became lovers. He has proposed innumerable times, but I like things the way they are. That is, until about two months ago. It was about then I began to notice that this affair is beginning to feel more like a marriage, and, I don't like that."

When a hot affair begins to seem more like a cool marriage, the difference may be because in an affair partners don't go to bed with each other's expectations. Mates seldom know what to expect in a torrid affair. Now that Larry and Sandi have become so close, Larry is beginning to anticipate her every desire. He already knows what Sandi thinks about most topics and how she will react during most situations. The excitement of anticipation is disappearing, fast. Sandi feels she has disclosed too much of herself. Nothing seems new or provocative to her in their relationship anymore–including the love song Larry sings to her each evening.

Since good sex takes place primarily in the mind, not the body, this couple's mindset needs stimulation. Part of the initial attraction between Larry and Sandi was the allure of the unknown. The desire to learn to know each other's tastes and behaviors is part of the fuel that fires a new relationship. Sandi is probably afraid of a maritial commitment because she will no longer have the feedom of action without considering her partner's needs. Maintaining a dynamic relationship with Larry or any partner requires thoughftulness and concentration. Most people don't like the idea of working hard in a relationship. Sandi is no exception. She wants the feelings of lust to last . . . effortlessly, just as Larry promised in the love songs he sings to her nightly. Larry assumes he knows all Sandi's wishes and desires. Sandi needs to change her responses and behave in unexpected ways. It's time for this couple to write some new lyrics together.

If couples put the same energy into making love exciting as they do into establishing and maintaining their careers, there would never be a shortage of sexual joy between them. It is true that even if a person adored hot fudge sundaes, he or she would quickly grow tired of them if he or she ate them every day. What seems delicious to a person on Saturday may not have any appeal on Wednesday. No one wants to eat the same thing all the time. Everyone likes variety. Why should the choice of sexual activities be any different?

As exciting as sex can be when it is new and fresh, sex in a marriage can never be like sex in an affair. There cannot be the same mystery or discovery as there is with a new lover. If partners engaged in the same intense passionate lovemaking over the long haul they would be dead, or at least exhausted. Because this is a culture obsessed with fantasy and staying forever young, when sexual passion fades, partners may feel they are being cheated.

Successful partners develop a sense of intimacy that no rush of sexual passion can equal. This sense of intimacy feels safe and comfortable, just like sex between loving partners becomes. When sexual blahs hit or one partner gets restless and lusts after someone new, it is easy to fantasize about entering another relationship.

What separates the successful relationships from the others is fidelity. This is the trust that partners develop in their commitment to the relationship. Almost every mate will look at other men and women and find them attractive just because these partners are still alive. It is normal to be attracted to other people. Although partners in successful relationships may look, they express their lust exclusively with each other. They do not give each other permission to become involved with other people when nothing seems to work between them sexually. It is true that almost every partner could find a better lover than the one with whom he or she is committed. It is a tremendous compliment mates give when they express their loyalty to each other. Most partners see the wisdom in repaying that loyalty.

All couples face sexual blahs. This is a given. Some people survive them by introducing sexual fantasy into the bedroom. Some partners act them out. Others just share their fantasies with their partners by talking about them. The most important thing to remember in a long-term relationship, or a short-term one a partner would like to extend, is to never stop trying to find new ways to interest a lover. What works today may work again next week.

CHAPTER 6

Dressing for Sexcess

There are very definite clothing fashions in sex. These fashions are not just found in stores like Frederick's of Hollywood or in tawdry sex salons. Most major department stores from Saks Fifth Avenue to J.C. Penny offer an extensive assortment of teddies, garter belts, and body stockings. The selections are voluminous, from luscious, vivid fuschia to sultry black, from delicate lace to slinky satin. Why are these items so readily available? Why do both men and women buy theses articles of clothing? The answer is that men are visually stimulated. They find sexy underwear and clothing both erotic and provocative.

At the same time, many women have a poor self-image about their bodies. In fact, most women feel very self-conscious and un-comfortable without their clothes on. A woman may view her bodily imperfections as glaring and distracting. She may compare herself to movie stars and models in fashion magazines and feel bad about her perceived shortcomings. It is difficult for a woman not to make such comparisons. Of course, no real woman looks that good in a photograph without brush strokes, no matter what her age. Feeling good about one's self and one's body is an important part of build-ing one's sexual confidence. Good communication skills can help couples deal better with these issues and lead to a more fulfilling sex life.

"Our anniversary was last Wednesday," Amy, a fifty-four-year-old housewife, was clearly exasperated. She began to describe a very frustrating experience that took place on the night that should have been very romantic.

"Arthur brought home a bottle of very expensive champagne. I had a surprise of my own. I had purchased a beautiful, pale mauve, very sheer, short nightgown. I had my hair done in a new, curly, provocative style. The hairdresser put a red rinse on it, so it was the same color as Maureen O'Hara's used to be. You know, that actress that used to co-star with John Wayne. Arthur always loved her in those movies. I was terribly nervous. We hadn't made love in months. Now that we have grandchildren, I spend a great deal of my time baby-sitting. When Arthur comes home from the store where he is an appliance salesman, he really doesn't want to talk much. Business is very competitive, now that there are so many discount stores. He is worn out trying to be pleasant and attentive to his customers. When he comes home, he just wants to be left alone. I am lucky if he compliments me on my meatloaf before he goes off to his den to watch TV.

"I have never had a strong sex drive. Arthur did for many years, but now that we have gotten older, he doesn't bother me so much. I thought I would give him a big surprise for our thirty-fourth wedding anniversary. Instead, I was the one who got the surprise.

"I had planned to put on the nightgown after dinner. Arthur walked through the door whistling, and put this bottle of champagne that we really couldn't afford in the refrigerator. I had prepared his favorite dinner. Arthur loves pork chops. I put candles on the table and used our good china. Everything looked very pretty. Because I didn't want to give away the surprise, I was dressed in what I usually wear when he comes home. I thought I looked very nice with my hair done in the new way.

"When dinner was over, Arthur said, 'Amy, I have a surprise for you.' I was expecting some new earrings. I had been hinting for them for weeks. Arthur produced a very large shopping bag from the town's best department store. In it was a black lace strapless bra and a garter belt with some flimsy black nylons with lace at the top. There was a skimpy pair of black panties and, believe it or not, a red wig! Yes, honestly! I shrieked at Arthur! How could he bring me something like that for an anniversary present? He knows I need an uplift bra and have put on a lot of weight in my hips over the last several years. Even if I could fit into the damn things, I'd look like a fat clown! Was he trying to make fun of me? I was outraged and then I began to cry. I told him about the beautiful nightgown I was planning to surprise him with when we went to bed. When Arthur looked at it, he said he thought it was pretty, but I knew he wanted to see me in something more sexy. The evening was ruined. We never did drink the champagne. If Arthur imagines I would ever wear something like those clothes after all these years, he really doesn't know me at all. Is my marriage over?"

As arousing as sexy negligees and provocative underwear can be to a partner, presenting them for the first time as a complete surprise can often produce a negative reaction. Sexual dressing can be exciting for a couple, but it cannot be introduced in a vacuum. If a partner goes to bed every night with rollers in her hair, wearing torn pajamas, a man cannot expect that she will not be offended when he suddenly produces a sexy outfit, expecting her to turn into a love goddess on the spot. Getting there, like all sexual expression, needs good communication between partners. If a couple has not had sex in months, they need to build up gradually to the grand climax.

Amy needed to rethink the romantic aspect of her marriage. If she wanted to have sex with her husband, she needed to create a sexual atmosphere. It was obvious that Arthur was still sexually interested in her, otherwise he would not have taken the time and trouble to purchase intimate clothing for her. Amy was concerned and embarrassed because she knew she no longer looked the way she had when Arthur and she first met. In Arthur's eyes, Amy was still desirable. He did not notice the added pounds in the same way she did. Lovers tend to see their mates through rose-colored glasses, which is why sex between a couple can continue well into old age. Sex has to do with feelings. Wrinkles and bulges often have little to do with sexual appetite.

Amy had been particularly upset because Arthur had purchased the red wig. It was important to point out to her that even *she* was aware of how much Arthur loved her hair when it was red. Hadn't she had it tinted that very afternoon in order to look more enticing to him?

Amy needs to think of herself as a more sexual person. This is where sexual dressing can be a big help. If Amy were to replace her everyday practical navy slacks with a soft, swinging, long skirt and exchange the cotton T-shirts she usually wears for flattering silk blouses, she would probably feel more feminine. Her attire would help create a more romantic atmosphere for sexual arousal to occur. Certainly her mauve nightgown would be an improvement over the flannel pajamas she usually wore. Gradually, Amy might enjoy discovering the gorgeous colors in the satin and silk lingerie offered by Victoria's Secret or a similar store. If Amy were too uncomfortable to purchase these items in a store, she could order them from a mail-order catalog, where she could make her selections in private.

It is important to remember that as a woman ages, her body requires more enhancement. The sensual feel of satin pajamas against a man's fingertips will feel much more pleasant to him than that of flannel pajamas. It is important for a partner to change her bedroom attire as she ages. Just as she would no longer wear the miniskirt and tube top she wore at seventeen, a woman needs to be aware of what is flattering to her charms as she ages.

FOR ADULTS ONLY!
Cathy and Lex were newlyweds. They had been together since high school. Although they attended different universities, it was clear they would marry as soon as they felt financially stable. When Cathy came for her first appointment, her eyes were red and her nails were bitten short. Her hair was tied back in a pony tail and her jeans and sneakers were torn. Though this was the current fashion among the very young, her attire was disconcerting.

> "Lex and I have always known we would marry. I dated other boys for a while and I'm certain he saw other girls, but we always knew we loved each other. Because we went to school in different cities, our lovemaking was confined to brief reunions on vacations and holidays. We never lived together before our marriage. It was exciting to see each other after being apart for so long. I don't know if Lex was a good lover or not. Sex was just the natural manifestation of our feelings. It seemed very comfortable to me.
>
> "Our wedding was small and very beautiful. Afterward, though, we were both exhausted. We really enjoyed the warm Florida sunshine and the beautiful blue water on our honeymoon. When we returned, Lex started to work in a small firm

and I went back to complete my final year of law school. Now I am studying for the bar exam. I admit, I'm tired and cranky most of the time.

"Neither of us comes from a wealthy family. When we were growing up, there was never any extra money for either of us to enjoy places we might want to go, like rock concerts, or to buy the current fashions the rest of our friends were wearing. Neither of us has ever experienced a very active social life. The extent of our world of entertainment was church suppers and interfaith camp. My wardrobe is mostly jeans which gets me by while I am in school and studying for the bar. Lex needed to buy a few suits when he began working at this firm. I've never cared about fashion and I didn't think Lex did either.

"Lately we have been invited to several parties. Some young couples from the firm have had us to dinner. Of course, there was the client Christmas party and one or two weddings we were invited to attend. I have a good black dress and some nice low-heeled suede pumps. That's all I've ever really needed for special occasions. When the last party invitation arrived, I told Lex I needed something new to wear. We had a big fight over money. I ended up borrowing a dress from one of my girl-friends. It was red—not my color. And the hemline was too short. I really didn't feel comfortable in it, but at least it was something new. Our friends complimented me on how I looked, but I knew they were just being polite. Then, Lex was sent to Chicago on a business trip. When he returned, he brought me a filmy yellow nightgown and a matching silk robe. It must have cost a fortune. I was furious. How could he spend money on something like this, when I had nothing to wear to his office functions?

"Lex told me he didn't care how I looked for other people. He just didn't want to go to bed with a woman who still slept in a gray sweatshirt. I felt he was bored with me. He knew what I was like when he married me. I am a very sensible person who likes to be comfortable. Why, after so short a time, is he trying to change me into something I'm not?"

Keeping yourself in good physical condition and caring about how you look to your partner is very important in a relationship. Cathy needed to be aware that how she looked was essential to how her mate viewed her. Lex was working in an environment where he saw other attractive women every day. He felt stimulated by the women he saw. His interest in Cathy needed to be aroused as well. If Cathy were to experiment by buying some new clothes, changing her hairstyle, and perhaps even trying a new cologne, Lex's interest in her would be rejuvenated. Cathy placed her comfort above her husband's desire to see her as more sexually alive. Although money was tight, they needed to discuss what each partner's needs were and to compromise on how they could satisfy those needs.

It is difficult for many young people to realize that what is attractive in a college setting sometimes seems childlike in an adult world. Cathy's serious, hardworking attitude toward life is commendable, but needs to be balanced with a more loving approach in the bedroom. Cathy needs to ignite Lex's interest by seeing her in new and different ways.

Money is often a problem for many newly married couples, but new hairstyles and pretty nightgowns need not cost a fortune. Sweatshirts might have been great for the girls in the dorm, but most men want to make love to an adult woman. Cathy needs to be more creative. For instance, cooking dinner in a frilly apron and nothing else would make absolutely no dent in their budget.

DRESSING FOR SEXCESS

Most women would not dream of going to a job interview dressed inappropriately. Presenting a positive image in the working world says that you are in focus. The world reacts accordingly. People look at such a woman with admiration and interest, trust and respect. A woman, in turn, reacts as any human being does when she is treated as a special person. She becomes more interesting and more worthy of that admiration, trust, and respect. Are these not the same reactions women want from their mates? Don't all women want to be treated as though they are very special? Yet some of the same women who could not imagine themselves showing up for work in something torn, messy, or unflattering, think nothing of going to bed in an old T-shirt her husband wore in college.

"Doesn't Tom realize I am tired?" exploded Linda, thirty-one, the very sexy looking young woman inhabiting the only soft, comfortable chair in the office. She began to rattle off her complaints.

"I am up at 6:00 a.m. every day. First, I make the coffee. Then I straighten the apartment. Tom usually makes the toast and brings in the paper. I read over my notes for the current ad campaign that I'm working on. I usually scribble some ideas on the pad I keep next to our bed during the night. I'm a terrible sleeper. I'm under great stress most of the time, but I don't know how I could live without it. I like having to stretch my creativity. I try to pace myself and not overload all my circuits. If the truth be known, I work much better when I'm under stress.

"Last Thursday, when I got home, Tom had already started dinner. He does that sometimes. I was exhausted, as usual. I took a quick shower and put on my favorite T-shirt. It's one that Tom wore when he played basketball in college. I put on a pair of his big, soft, athletic socks, grabbed a drink from the fridge, and started reading the paper on the couch in the living room. I never have time to read it in the morning. Tom slammed the skillet he was using on the stove. He *threw* the corkscrew for the wine he had chilling across the kitchen. Then, he *screamed* at me that I should call my sister, Ellen, to come over to eat the damn dinner. *He* was going out!

"I had no idea what had gotten into him. He loves to cook and often makes a gourmet dinner. I love to relax in something old and comfortable. He knows I am usually too tired for sex during the week. What did he want? What did he expect?"

ROLE REVERSAL

It used to be that if a woman slaved all day over a hot stove preparing dinner to please her husband, she would be very upset if he came home, gave her a peck on the cheek, ate the dinner, and then went off to read his newspaper or watch television. In today's world, many marriages have two bread-winning partners. Each is well educated. Each is equally intense in pursuing a career. Because many women work in the same competitive, stress-filled world today, they certainly expect their partner to assume his part of the responsibilities in the marriage. But Linda had not realized that when Tom came home from the office, he wanted to find a sexual partner there, not just an exhausted person who looked like his old college roommate.

Linda needed to understand that her boss would not be pleased if she arrived at the office looking like a frump. Her clients would find her less than appealing or professional. Why should her husband expect anything less? Tom's preparation of the dinner was a prelude to romance. He was trying to create a loving atmosphere in which they both might express themselves sexually. Linda's attire was a turn-off. Would she have liked his sweat socks next to her in bed? How would Linda have responded to Tom returning from work and expecting her to provide all the personal attention in their marriage?

Tom and Linda's marriage is suffering badly from stagnation. They are in a sexual rut. Linda needs to create some sexual interest and show Tom that he is just as important to her as any client. If she wants his attention, she needs to create sparks. One way Linda could create some sexual interest in her marriage is for her to begin dressing for sexcess. She could create play clothes for the time when she and Tom are alone. When Tom prepares the dinner, perhaps she could play salad chef. An attractive apron over a black lace bra and panties might add even more seasoning to their dinner than the salad dressing itself. Perhaps she could call it salad *un*dressing. Linda is an advertising whiz. If she wants Tom to buy her product, she needs to create some stimulating copy for herself and then act it out.

Linda might decide to give Tom a new photo for his office or their apartment, so that he could fantasize when they are separated during the day about what their evening together would be like. There are photo studios in every city that allow their clients to model sexy clothing from an extensive studio supply. Tantalizing hairstyles and sexy poses are captured in color photographs for a woman to give to her lover. These portrait studios are listed in the yellow pages, usually as glamour or love photography.

PAPER DOLL

One of the cleverest ideas for dressing for sexcess came from Emily, a "thritysomething" pediatrician. Emily and John had been married for seven years and had two small children. The children were in day care while their parents were at work. John sold insurance. He worked long hours and most evenings. Their leisure time together was limited. Even vacations were spent with their children. The last vacation was at Disneyland, not a place one would consider an intimate sexual paradise. But on this particular trip John had purchased an entire wardrobe for Emily to wear. Every outfit was composed of low-cut, tight-fitting knit tops and micro miniskirts. Although Emily wouldn't be caught dead wearing these clothes at home where people knew her, in the vacationland surroundings where no one recognized them, they both found Emily's outfits sexually exciting. Emily's behavior was more teasing and playful when she was wearing this suggestive clothing. John could hardly wait until they were alone together, after the children were in bed in their own room with a sitter to watch them, where there were no interruptions.

John and Emily now plan their vacations this way. They peruse the brochures just as everyone else does, choosing the points of interest they will be visiting during the day. They select fabulous restaurants and ponder over the best rates for rental cars. But Emily's wardrobe changes with the destination. John purchases most of these outfits in discount stores so as not to exhaust their budget. They are looking forward to a trip to San Francisco without the children. In a city so diverse, one can only imagine what erotic outfits John will find for Emily.

SIZZLE ON STAGE
Jane entered therapy when she discovered her lover of eight months seemed to be cooling toward her. Jane and her lover, Riley, were married— to other people. They had met through a local theater group when several couples from their church decided to include performing in the rapidly growing list of activities that was being offered. Riley and Jane auditioned together, with the approval and blessing of both their spouses. Riley's wife, Clara, was happy he had found a new interest. He seemed to be bored so easily. Pete had always been proud of Jane's acting ability. They had met in college while each worked on the school's production of *Hamlet*.

Rehearsals and production involved many hours each week. By the time the first play had been performed to glowing local reviews, the theater group was well on its way to becoming a permanent part of the community arts scene. It was this seemingly "safe" setting that Jane and Riley first became attracted to each other. Jane, whose marriage of ten years had always been rocky, couldn't help but enjoy the interest Riley showed in her. He helped her with her lines and gave her confidence. Her former existence as a housewife and mother seemed to fade into the background. Jane's total life was now absorbed in the time she and Riley could spend together.

"In that first play in which Riley and I co-starred, I was cast as a smoldering sex symbol. My costumes included a silver lamé jumpsuit and a red, skin-tight, low-cut, backless evening gown. In one scene, I was disguised as a French maid. All of these costumes felt strange to me. They were completely different from anything I wore in my real life as a wife and mother. I actually did seem to take on the feelings and characteristics of the sex symbol I was portraying. The response I got from Riley made me feel something I had never felt before: sexually potent. I could command sexual interest. Me! Imagine! It was a heady experience. Riley had not known me as the tame "little good girl" personality I had manifested before we began acting together. He responded to me as I looked and behaved in these parts. I loved it. I felt so free and tantalizing.

"Even planning the times when Riley and I could be together took on the quality of theater. We didn't want to leave our spouses, so we were very careful about how often and where we met. The funny part of it was that when my persona changed with each part I played, my husband seemed more interested in me, too. I lost my previous inhibitions. Although I was still concerned about hurting Pete, and I certainly was aware that what Riley and I were doing was morally wrong, ultimately I gave in to the passionate feelings I felt with Riley. The thrill and excitement of being able to attract another person seemed paramount to fulfilling some emotional need of mine that had previously lain dormant. The romantic atmosphere in which we found ourselves was thrilling."

"Three weeks ago, I was cast in a new part. I play a bitchy alcoholic who is unable to establish relationships with men or with her own child. I feel great in the part. Everyone feels I will win the award for best actress in a local theater group this year. My husband is proud of the way I have grown as a performer. He shared that he had always been embarrassed watching me on stage when I was playing the role of a tramp. Pete may be proud, but Riley is showing strong interest in the beautiful little blond playing the role of the ingenue. I see them together. He is helping her with her lines. She has seven in the entire play!

"The amazing part of all of this is that I am not terribly unhappy the affair is ending. I found it difficult to lie to my family and friends. It was very unpleasant to always feel so guilty. Even the sex with Riley was becoming a bit boring. But, sex with Pete has its limitations, too. How can I get some of the sizzle I felt with Riley back into my own marriage?"

Pete may have felt uncomfortable watching Jane perform as a vamp in front of other people, but it might turn him on if she were to give him a private performance. By Jane's own account, she felt and acted more sexual when she was able to pretend she was someone else. She found the costumes and atmosphere of make-believe freeing to her sexually. She also found that she was very good at playing the role of another person. Perhaps Jane might try to incorporate some of her talent into her marriage. She could convince Pete to join in some personal theater. Jane now knows how to do props and makeup. She also understands their value. By including Pete in an intimate drama, their sex life might turn out to be even more exhilarating than the high Jane receives performing before strangers. Hers is a talent Pete greatly admires. Putting that talent into action for an audience of one could be just the thing to rejuvenate a stale marriage. Riley, by all observations, will probably go on to one leading lady after another. Jane and Pete could make the run of their production excel even that of *Cats*.

When relationships become rocky, it can be tempting to seek approval and fulfillment from someone else. This new person may only see the role presented, without the faults and flaws a partner finds so irritating. It takes most couples long periods of time through many difficult situations to form a true loving relationship. This investment of trust and deep caring is called commitment. No sexual relationship can successfully endure without a continuing pledge of confidence and responsibility to each other. A change of costume can be fun and exhilarating. Commitment to a partner needs to be constant and requires love and tenderness deep enough to penetrate the most artistic makeup and artifice.

IMAGINATION IS THE GREATEST GIFT

Many years ago there was a romantic song sung by a pretty, bubbly vocalist named Doris Day, the typical virginal girl next door. When she sang about her imagination, no one imagined anything more sensual than an all-white wedding and a group of giggling bridesmaids gathered around an adoring groom. For better or for worse, times have changed. Now, a couple's imagination is what is needed to keep a marriage crackling. Imagination costs nothing. Everyone has one. It is an unlimited commodity. The more an imagination is exercised, the greater the personal reward. It can be the most challenging adventure of a couple's life to keep each other sexually aroused and erotically involved. Planning to infuse a marriage with sizzle and keep it romantic can be a wonderful pastime for any couple. Don't forget how enjoyable it was to play dress up as children. Choosing different clothing was helpful in being able to play "let's pretend." Just because a person grows older does not mean the same games cannot be enjoyed.

CHAPTER 7

Say Something Nice or Nothing at All

Giving and receiving criticism is often one of the most frequent trouble spots for a couple's relationship. Sexual criticism is decidedly the most difficult to voice to a lover and is certainly the most devastating to hear. When a partner makes critical or hurtful remarks, both in and out of bed, it negatively affects sexual desire. Criticism about sexual skills makes a mate feel inadequate. Even when the criticism is sincerely meant to be constructive, it can be felt as very unkind. Harsh, insensitive comments often cause angry feelings that overpower feelings of warmth and lust. These kinds of comments, especially when they are deliberately cruel, can scar and even ruin a sexual relationship. Yet, at one time or another, most mates criticize each other. How can partners learn to express preference or displeasure without hurting each other and damaging their relationship?

Many a woman wonders why the man who claimed to love her desperately and said he could not imagine a life without her suddenly decides that everything she does is wrong. Usually the complaints are hiding other feelings. It is important for every couple to share their feelings honestly, but when criticism begins to destroy a sexual relationship, it is time to take action. Lisa's story is an example of how devastating critical remarks can be.

> "David and I have been together for only a few months. This is not the first sexual relationship for either of us. David is no kid. He is forty-two. I will be thirty on my next birthday. We met at

a sports bar — a bar isn't necessarily the best place to meet future partners, but we both enjoy sports and met through some mutual friends during the play-offs last year. David is a very attractive man. He works as a sportswriter for the local paper. He knows everyone. He has traveled a great deal and knows how to treat a lady. He orders for me in restaurants and brings me flowers. When he recently made a killing in the stock market, David took me shopping for a new summer wardrobe. I always feel special when I am with him. No man has treated me this way before. I find him exciting and unpredictable. He is a good lover in bed. I was hoping he would ask me to marry him.

"A few weeks ago, David's attitude toward me began to change. We had taken a brief vacation together. David needed to cover preseason training and he asked me to come along. I spent the days at the hotel gym working out and taking saunas. I exercise whenever I can. I am very proud of my body, so I take good care of it. That evening we had a wonderful dinner together. Then we joined some of the guys on the team in the hotel lobby to discuss the coming season. I was getting a little impatient and was hoping David would say goodnight and come to bed for a little sexual activity. I nibbled at his ear and kept my arm around him, stroking his back and shoulders while he continued to kibitz with the guys. Finally, he said we had to be going and we went to our room. I began to unbutton his shirt and run my fingers through the hairs on his chest. He usually loves when I play with his body. David pulled away abruptly and began complaining about my sexual teasing in front of his friends. He doesn't like public displays of affection. I know that, but it is hard for me to keep my hands off him. I apologized immediately and thought the incident was over. Then, the very next evening, when we were in bed, David commented that I was gaining weight. He suggested I lay off the desserts for a while. When I challenged his remark by reminding him I exercised almost daily, he retaliated by suggesting that my breasts were too small. I was crushed. I've always taken such pride in my body. David has told me repeatedly how much he likes the way I look and how much he enjoys my enthusiasm for sex.

"Then, last night, right out of the blue, he told me that I was the most sexually aggressive woman with whom he had ever been involved. It was not said as a compliment. I hate to be compared to his former lovers. When we are together, I like to believe there has never been anyone else for either of us. I was so hurt, I got dressed and left his apartment. He hasn't called. How can I keep from losing him? How can I learn to accept his criticism?"

WHEN WHAT YOU SAY IS NOT WHAT YOU MEAN

Several things were going on in this relationship. David was obviously upset with Lisa, but instead of telling her the real reason for his annoyance, he criticized her sexuality. Lisa could not accept his negative remarks, but was too afraid of David's rejection to see his words for what they might have really meant.

David had suggested the brief trip because he saw it as a time for getting to know each other better. Lisa's cloying of David's body in front of his buddies made him feel as though he was her possession, not her escort. When Lisa stroked his body in public, she was giving a nonverbal message to his friends that David already belonged to her. David was feeling trapped in a relationship to which he had not yet decided he wanted to commit. Instead of telling Lisa how he was still thinking about where this relationship might be going, David panicked. He criticized Lisa in her most vulnerable area, her body of which she was so proud. Most likely, he felt she would be so devastated, *she* would break off the relationship, relieving *him* of the responsibility.

Lisa has some options. Since her feelings for David seem to be stronger than his for her at this time, she might invite him for a quick drink. Dinner at her apartment would seem too threatening to him. Meeting for a drink would mean there is a set time limit. It also means talking in a public place so David need not fear Lisa would become too emotional and make a scene. That would cause David to feel even more uncomfortable and less likely to want to see her again in any setting.

When they are together, Lisa could be honest with David about her feelings without causing him to feel guilty. Since they are *her feelings* she needs to take responsibility for them. Lisa could ask him to tell her what he wants so that she knows where she stands. She should not, however, sacrifice her own wants and needs in order to please him. Lisa could tell David that he delights her greatly, both in and out of bed. She can make it clear that she cares enough about him to listen to what is bothering him. If David can be honest with Lisa, he will tell her his feelings—probably that he dislikes her possessiveness and feels he is suffocating in the relationship. Perhaps then they can discuss a way for Lisa to back off and give him some breathing space. Lisa could explain to David that when he criticizes her breasts, there is almost nothing she can do about it, short of plastic surgery. Criticizing her physical attributes and her sexual appetite is malicious and counter-productive. If David decides to try to continue this relationship, perhaps he could learn to cushion his preferences in words such as "I love your enthusiasm for sex, but I prefer you confine your display of affection for when we are alone. I feel uncomfortable showing my sexual feelings in public."

It is important for all couples to state what they want in a positive manner. Emphasize the pleasure your partner gives you. State what you wish changed by saying such things as, "I love the way you touch me when we are alone together," rather than by saying "I hate when you stroke my body in public." It is possible that David does not really know why he became so angry with Lisa. If partners can help each other verbalize their feelings without attacking one another in a cruel and destructive manner, their relationship will have a greater opportunity to succeed.

PREVIOUS EXPERIENCE NOT REQUIRED
Tiffany, a fabulous-looking blond, had an extremely sensitive problem.

> "Zack and I met at art school about two years ago. I was posing for his life drawing class in order to earn some extra money to help me between modeling jobs. They are few and far between in this city, although I suppose I've been luckier than most. A furrier used me for most of his print advertising and I did a lot of runway modeling for local department stores. I was hoping to earn enough money to go to New York, but then I met Zack, and everything changed.
>
> "Zack is the son of a very wealthy car dealer here in town. His parents move in prominent social circles. His mother is constantly being photographed and interviewed for the society pages of our local newspapers and magazines. When I first met him, Zack was taking this class in illustration while he was

home from college for the summer. He has a little talent and likes to try lots of things. Last winter he took a course in pottery and now our apartment is littered with brochures for a creative writing class being offered in the fall.

"You could say he fell in love with me at first sight. I was a little more cautious. After that first class, he asked if he could buy me a beer. I declined, because I had an early call to model the next day. Besides, I really don't care for beer. I guess he thought I was intriguing, so he asked the instructor for my telephone number. From that night on, he left all kinds of funny messages on my answering machine. I would come home to hear things like 'Didn't I just see your picture on the cover of *Vanity Fair*? You really didn't look pregnant in class the other night.' Of course, he was referring to the nude photo of a pregnant Demi Moore on the magazine's cover that year. Sometimes the message would just be to call him within the next few months. He said he was used to waiting in the bakery line for his number to come up. Little things, but he said them so endearingly. I began to look forward to receiving those messages.

"As fall drew nearer, Zack planned to go back to school. I was no longer modeling for his class. There was really no reason to see each other. I never did return any of his calls. Then, one evening, I was modeling for a charity fashion show his mother was chairing. The first time I walked down the runway, I saw Zack, who began applauding loudly. It was embarrassing. When the show was over, Zack jumped onto the stage to present me with the gorgeous roses that were meant for his mother. She took it most graciously. She bowed to me, just as he did, and they both escorted me off the stage. I was so flustered, I didn't know what to say. He insisted I join his parents and their friends at the head table. Too humiliated to refuse them, I did. Everyone was so kind to me. They seemed very interested in my career. Zack's father even asked me to dance.

"After that auspicious beginning, Zack and I began to date regularly. He never stopped telling me how beautiful I was. He brought me wonderful presents and took me to exciting clubs and parties. Imagine my surprise when he informed me the he had transferred to the local university. He said it was better for him. This school had an excellent marketing department. Zack felt he could work for his father after classes so that he would really know the business when he graduated the following year.

"Zack treated me better than anyone ever had before. He was sweet and attentive and supportive of my career. His family knew all the local store owners and soon I had more modeling jobs than I could handle. When we made love, he was thoughtful and considerate. Zack was my first lover and everything seemed new and exciting. I had a great deal of difficulty in reaching a climax—in fact, most of the time I never did. But, when I told this to Zack, he seemed disappointed in me, so I didn't mention it again. He would constantly ask me if what he was doing was right. Was it too fast? Was it too slow? How did I know? I began to wonder if there was something wrong with me.

"By this time, everyone was asking when we were going to be married. Graduation was just a few months away. Even his mother suggested we plan a June wedding. Then, for Valentine's day, three days before my birthday, Zack presented me with boots and skis for a weekend in Aspen. I knew what they were by the shape of the packages. I was so thrilled, I kissed him before I opened them. Zack insisted I try the ski boots on immediately. Imagine my surprise when my foot felt something in the bottom of the boot. It was a diamond ring! I thought I was in paradise.

"Things happened very quickly after that. His mother took me shopping for a gown. I chose the one I had recently modeled in a bridal show. Our ceremony and reception seemed like a fairy tale. I had never seen so many beautiful flowers. The chapel was filled with pale apricot roses. My three bridesmaids wore exquisite gowns with straw picture hats and silk shoes. They carried baskets overflowing with apricot roses, and ivory orchids. Even my friends told me our wedding was like taking part in a dream. The wedding gifts were fantastic too. My father-in-law gave us a new car. My mother-in-law gave me the use of her decorator and a large check for our new apartment. Everything seemed to be just perfect.

"Zack began to work for his father immediately after graduation. I was not working nearly as often. Decorating the apartment and planning wonderful little suppers for Zack became my all-consuming priorities. Then, little things began to happen. I had always been a bit shy in the bedroom. I had read several books on sex that I bought in bookstores, but what they suggested seemed silly to me. I still was unable to reach a climax most of the time. Zack wanted to have sex with me almost every night. Although I had succumbed on our honeymoon, I really thought he was oversexed. Didn't normal people have sex just twice a week? Zack began to get very irritable. If I didn't have a climax, he thought it was his fault. I began to dodge his kisses and avoid any of his overtures to making love. All I could think of was, what if I don't please him? What if I can never have an orgasm? I don't want Zack to leave me, but he criticizes me so often now for being frigid, I'm afraid that he will."

RICHES MONEY CAN'T BUY

Even when everything else seems perfect, couples who have unrealistic expectations about sex can feel their relationship is bankrupt. Many people believe that everyone else is having fantastic sex every night of the week. If they are not, they may start to feel inadequate and criticize themselves or their mates. When partners criticize their mate's sexuality they are really attacking their self-esteem. This criticism hits where a partner is most vulnerable. No one is born knowing how to make love. No one is *born* knowing almost *anything*.

We study to learn our professions. We take lessons to comprehend the latest dance steps. We must read and experiment to learn how to cook, how to drive, how to play cards. Why, then, do we often assume we do not have to learn how to make love? Remember the charming story of Colette's Gigi? Even a captivating woman like Gigi had to be taught to become a courtesan.

When Zack criticized Tiffany's sexuality, it was obvious he did not have accurate information about human sexuality. Zack needs to know that the capacity for orgasm varies greatly from woman to woman. Some women have a great desire for sex, and yet have difficulty in reaching arousal. If Zack and Tiffany are able to trust each other's love, they might be able to discuss the various ways Zack might try to stimulate her. Tiffany might take Zack's fingers, when they begin to make love and guide them gently to show him what feels good to her. If Tiffany would demonstrate to Zack what she would like him to do by her response, Zack might feel more comfortable with his own lovemaking. When words are too abrasive, action can be very effective.

Tiffany needs to take more responsibility for her own sexual arousal. She needs to forget her sexual expectations for the time being and take the time to explore her own body. Once she discovers what feels good to her, she will be able to show Zack. If Tiffany suggests to Zack that they explore their sexual feelings together at their own pace, he might then become excited at the idea of discovering what turns Tiffany on. With less pressure on them both, they will be able to enjoy sex more and give each other a gift no money could buy.

It is not possible for on person to make another feel sexy. This is something one can only do for one's self. Zack was first attracted to Tiffany because she was totally involved in activities that fulfilled and excited her. This energy was then translated into a kind of sexual aura. Because Tiffany was happy with herself, she was able to appreciate Zack's generous spirit and supportiveness. Zack, in turn, felt loved and fulfilled. Zack showed his love by easing some of Tiffany's responsibilities and helping her to be more economically productive. He was interested in Tiffany's personal growth, just as he was in his own. This was illustrated by his continuous involvement in classes that enriched his life. When Tiffany married, she became totally involved in pleasing Zack, from her sexual performance in the bedroom to her culinary achievements in the kitchen. Although she was certainly expressing her love for Zack in these ways, she had lost the very qualities Zack loved about her. He saw her as a beautiful, adventurous woman who satisfied her own ambitions and needs. To Zack, she was a woman with a goal of becoming a model in New York. Tiffany needs to resume living her own life, for herself as well as for Zack. Then, they could continue to share that energy together.

Tiffany had mentioned the numerous books on sex that she purchased. Although many of these books are helpful, they generally concentrate on technique instead of on feelings. Tiffany needs to give herself *permission* to feel love. Like that wonderful television commercial for hair coloring, she needed to feel that she is worth it! Perhaps, alone in the privacy of her bedroom, Tiffany could try a vibrator and learn to bring herself to orgasm. Then, when she feels more comfortable with her own feelings of receiving pleasure, she could ask Zack to stroke her body in places she knows feel good to her. Tiffany needs to trust that Zack will not criticize or make fun of her if she shows her vulnerability. Zack needs to praise Tiffany for trying to find the mutual sexual satisfaction they both so greatly desire.

CHANGE YOUR CRITCAL MATE

Sometimes mates who have difficulty expressing their true emotions use criticism to protect themselves from individual feelings of inadequacy and vulnerability. If a man is able to point out his wife's shortcomings, he may feel better about himself. Similarly, if a woman unfairly criticizes her partner, she is able to maintain emotional distance from him and not become vulnerable. It is particularly difficult when relationships are overshadowed by constant criticism. Often mates do not realize when this mode of relating starts to erode all other aspects of the relationship.

"Twenty-two years of marriage, and he hasn't learned a thing! I can't stand it anymore. I've tried everything. All Joe does is criticize, from his first words in the morning, when he complains about the delivery boy leaving our paper in the driveway until we are getting ready for bed and he can't find the socks he wants to wear the next day. He is as stubborn as a mule. I don't want to leave him, but I think I'll have to. I've had it with his criticism.

"Joe thinks that I am overweight. I have weighed the same since we were first married, but it's shifted around some and the styles have changed. Thin is in. I was never thin. I wear a size twelve and have since I was in school. Joe is constantly cutting out diets from magazines and newspapers and leaving them for me to read. Whenever we go out, he talks about how svelte the other women are and how great they look. They are not *all* thin, but he doesn't seem to notice that. He criticizes what I order, how I look, and what I do.

"Joe also complains about my business. I have started a small employment agency which I run out of our house, primarily for part-time secretarial and household help. I meet a lot of interesting people, and feel like I'm serving a useful purpose. Earning the extra money also allows me to spoil our children a bit. The girls always want new clothes or extras now that they are away in college. Our older son is married and lives in another state. When I buy these little gifts, I don't have to listen to Joe criticize me for spending too much money when the charges come in each month. I can go a little overboard at Christmas and buy a few things I want for our house. It makes me feel more independent. But all Joe does is complain about how much time my business takes away from my cleaning the house, doing the laundry, or going bowling with him. At least I am not asking *him* for the money."

In her opinion, Sharon had exhausted all her options to change Joe. After so many years of listening to his criticism, she felt she could no longer tolerate his judgmental remarks.

"About a month ago, we had some friends over for dinner. I planned a picnic in the backyard, but I wanted to make it special. I used all my best china, silver, and crystal on a white damask cloth my mother had given us for our wedding. I hadn't used these beautiful things in so long. The garden looked almost mystical in the candlelight. Our friends were delighted with my unusual preparations and everyone complimented me on my ingenuity. Everyone, that is, except Joe. He was furious. He complained I had risked breaking the crystal glasses that had been in the family for generations by using them outside. He thought the damask cloth under platters of grilled salmon and green salad was ridiculous, if not ostentatious. He felt I was reducing family heirlooms to frivolity, and that I was trying to show off for our friends. I explained how I was trying to create a romantic setting and that the crystal was in no more danger of being broken or the silver lost than they would be in our dining room. The party was almost ruined for me before the guests arrived and restored faith in my creativity. Joe was still in an angry mood during dinner. He chose during the dessert of fresh strawberries and cream fraise to complain how I was so busy in my business, I didn't have time to bake a pie. Then he suggested I not have the topping on my strawberries, since I had indulged in the dill sauce on my salmon and eaten several of the buttered muffins.

"The final straw came Saturday night after a particularly sexy video Joe had brought home. We were watching the film in the family room with our next-door neighbors. Wow, was it hot. I could hardly wait until they left, so that I could seduce Joe like the actress had done to her lover on screen. After washing the glasses and popcorn bowl in the kitchen, I slunk into the family room unbuttoning my blouse as I entered and thrusting out my chest so Joe could get a glimpse of my lacy red bra. I had been saving it and the matching red bikini pants for an occasion like this.

"Joe scowled and said, 'What do you think you're doing?'

"'Just thought I'd try to give you a little loving,' I responded, making a great effort to overlook his disapproving tone of voice.

"'Look, Sharon, I've just spent almost two hours watching a gorgeous babe strip and gyrate. How do you think I can respond to an overweight housewife after that?'"

WHEN LOVE BECOMES WAR

Cruel? You bet. Yet how many men are insensitive to their partners in much the same way? Many women respond with anger or tears. Some threaten to leave, just as Sharon had done many times before. But most people seem to respond best when they are dealt with as an adults—even when they are not acting like one. Sharon had tried intimidation and condescension. She had even tried to belittle Joe in front of others, just as he had done to her. But her efforts only made things worse, until there was a constant state of warfare between them. Joe retaliated by constantly criticizing everything Sharon did. It was important for Sharon to realize he criticized almost everyone else as well. If Sharon wanted to stay in her marriage, she would need to find another way to deal with the situation.

When a mate constantly criticizes, he is angry with himself. Perhaps his job is not going as well as expected. Maybe success has been elusive. When money is tight and demands are increasing, of course there can be tension in a marriage. Sharon had gone to work to help out with the finances. Joe felt she was saying she could get along without him. Joe harped continuously on Sharon's weight, but perhaps there was some other aspect of her personality that was getting to him. Sharon was content with the way she looked. She was successful with her job. Her friends found her warm and trustworthy and her children loved her. Maybe Sharon needed to ignore Joe's constant badgering about her weight and concentrate on getting on with her life and enjoying it to the fullest. Sharon could develop an inner peace of mind and focus on what really matters to her. If Sharon's weight was indeed a health concern, perhaps she could be careful to maintain a healthy diet and exercise regularly. By making the attempt, she would be showing Joe that his concerns were important to her. By not trying, Joe felt Sharon was saying there was no way she was going to cooperate with his wishes.

It was obvious that this couple was playing "the control game," which sometimes does result in "the crying game." When Joe tried to dominate or control Sharon by his constant badgering, she responded by ignoring him or finding a new way to break free. If he criticized her weight, she planned opulent dinner parties to prove he could not control her. Partnership does not mean one mate controls the other. Partnership means equality. The person who feels less powerful often always sabotage a mate's attempts to dominate,

As difficult as it might be for Sharon, if she wants to change Joe's critical attitude, she needs to make him hear her. This is almost impossible, but not quite. Deborah Tannen's insightful book, *You Just Don't Understand*, discusses the problems men have listening to women. An outstanding psychologist, Tannen states it is a cultural inability in men, and probably in women, for them to hear each other. Men will nod, smile, but they do not listen. Even the first woman Supreme Court Justice, Sandra Day O'Conner, tells that when she wished for male colleagues to listen, she lowered her voice almost to a whisper so that they would have to strain to hear what she was saying. Sharon expected Joe to hear what she was saying. He only heard her tone and reacted to what she did, not what she said.

READ MY LIPS
It is imperative for Sharon, as it is for all partners, to find a way to make Joe listen. One way she could do this is by *acknowledging* Joe's *feelings* before she tells him how she feels. If Sharon simply says, "I was furious at the way you embarrassed me in front of our friends at our dinner party last month," Joe would probably say something like, "When I told you privately how I felt about your arrangements, you paid no attention to me and did as you pleased," and thus begins an argument. Instead, Sharon might say, "I am sorry. I know you were worried about the family crystal. I just wanted you to be impressed with all my hard work and creativity. I wanted you to think the party was different and fun. I would have liked your input and cooperation." Then, Joe would be responsible for acknowledging Sharon's point of view. After he had done so, he could ex-

plain how he felt about being left out of the planning of this festive evening.

It is likely that Joe would take responsibility for his role in this conflict if Sharon took responsibility for hers. When Joe dismisses Sharon's feelings as unimportant, she feels diminished and insignificant. But if Joe does not receive validation in his partner's eyes, he will try even harder to get her to see his point of view. And the war goes on and on. In order to stop the war of criticism, partners must each change themselves.

As difficult and destructive as criticism is to live with, a mate must carefully consider if the changes desired are really important. No one wants to live with someone so pliable as to respond to every whim and wish and overlook his or her own needs. Every person is an individual with a distinct personality. It is this very individualism that makes partners fall in love in the first place. Perhaps it is the measure of that love that determines what couples decide they *can* live with and what they cannot. Partners need to ponder why that change is needed and consider what is involved. When a mate feels as if his partner is taking his concerns into consideration, he will be less likely to criticize. Remember, partners do not change on demand. If they choose to change their behavior, it will only be done freely, as a gift of love.

CHAPTER 8

The Egg Timer Lover

It is not at all unusual to hear that some couples spend just five to ten minutes making love from start to finish. When both partners agree, "quickies" can be mutually satisfying. When only one partner, usually the male, determines how long lovemaking will last, the woman may be left wondering, Is that all there is? These overzealous men are like "egg timer lovers," trying to complete lovemaking before the sand runs through the egg timer. Love is done, like a three-minute egg. The man might be satisfied. What about his partner?

There are significant differences between having sex and making love. Studies show that most women want and need at least twenty to forty minutes of foreplay most of the time. That means twenty to forty minutes spent together in bed before intercourse begins. In addition, most women want some romance throughout the day and evening. Men are often unsure of their own sexual performance. They do not always know when a woman is ready for intercourse. A woman needs to tell her man in a caring way when she is physically ready.

There are a number of steps couples can take to improve their sex lives and increase that loving feeling, including foreplay. Foreplay is defined as everything a couple does all day and all night long. It really should be called *constant play* or *continuous play* because it goes on all day, both before and after sexual intercourse. Couples need to think of foreplay as getting in the mood and staying in the mood.

Sondra, thirty-eight and angry, described how her day usually began with a list of instructions for her from her husband, Ron. This list of "orders" put her in a bad mood for the rest of the day. When he wanted sex, she felt resentful.

"Before Ron left for the office this morning, he leaned over the bed and said, 'Don't spend any money today. This house we are building is costing a fortune. I don't have anything left over to pay for your charge accounts. Oh, and don't forget to call the builder and find out when he will begin to tile the bathrooms.'

"He never even said, 'Have a nice day, honey' or, 'I hope the kids in your class don't give you too much of a hard time today.' He just told me not to spend any money and left. I felt annoyed and on edge for the rest of the day. I work very hard, too. I'm a second-grade teacher and that is not an easy job. The children are darling but demanding and challenging. I know constructing this house is expensive, but we made the decision together to build it. It's something we both want.

"The rest of my day didn't get much better. After a hectic day at school, I picked up our two young children from the sitter, went grocery shopping, made dinner, bathed the children, and read them a story before putting them to bed. Then I spoke to my mother on the phone, trying to raise her spirits. She is a recent widow and is very depressed. When Ron got home from his meeting at 10:00 p.m., I gave him a bite to eat. We were in bed by 11:00 p.m. watching the news when Ron leaned over and whispered to me that he wanted sex. I was about as much in the mood for sex as I was for mountain climbing. I was exhausted. He made me so angry. What am I? A pleasure machine?"

Understandably, Sondra wanted some attention and caring before Ron began making love to her. They were both exhausted. She understood that he was as tired as she. The difference was, she was still feeling angry with Ron for being made to feel like a servant when he gave her his list of orders in the morning. The fact that Ron had left the house without kissing her good-bye made it difficult for Sondra to have any great expectations about what might happen sexually later on in the evening. She was still very upset that he had made her feel so on edge for the entire day.

Much like the proverbial man who left audio-taped instructions for his wife to play while he was at the office, Ron seemed to have forgotten that she was his wife, not his servant. "Pick up my shirts.

Don't forget my shoes from the repair shop. Have the oil changed in the car today." If a lover behaved toward a woman in this way, she would not be too anxious to see him again. Sondra needs to tell Ron how she wishes to be treated so that she can respond lovingly to him.

DEFLECTING CRITICAL COMMENTS

When a man begins the day with a list of instructions for his wife, she can divert what is happening by saying something like "Good morning, honey. You really do look nice in that tie. I hope you have a good day." She does not need to become engaged in verbal combat. She does not want to get hooked into responding to his accusations with defensive words such as, "I do not spend too much money." This is a no-win situation. She needs to change the whole focus to something positive and pleasant.

It's important for her to also acknowledge his feelings. For example, Sondra might tell Ron she understands he is under a lot of financial pressure with the construction of the new house, but she hopes he will have a nice day, or that his sales meeting will go well (or that they win the lottery).

At a calmer time, Sondra could suggest to Ron that, before he leaves for work, they say only nice things to each other to set a positive tone for the day. She could propose that if he wants a chore done, he might leave a note in the kitchen with the requests softened by a, "Would you please," or "If you get the chance . . ." She could suggest he sign these notes with an endearment, such as, "I love you," or, "I hope your day goes well." Sondra needs to tell Ron how much softer and warmer she will feel toward him when he leaves her for the day with a kiss instead of a battery of commands. Ron could also call her during the day to say he is thinking of her, which would certainly make Sondra feel Ron is a caring lover.

When couples reunite at the end of the day, it is helpful not to greet each other with, "Oh, what a horrible day!" or to report everything that went wrong during the day. Couples often feel they can dump their emotional garbage on their mate the moment they walk through the door. This behavior does not create a loving, sexual, atmosphere. A woman needs to ask her man not to greet her by telling her he is so tired he can hardly move, even if it is true. She should ask him not to tell her that all he wants is to be left alone. These words are not conducive to making wild, passionate love. They are conducive to making her want to dump the dinner on his head. Or it may make her feel sorry for him, but it certainly won't make her feel sexy toward him. Of course, these same rules apply to her as well.

At a pleasant time together outside the bedroom, Sondra could explain to Ron that, although he may not realize it, what he says to her in the morning will affect her hours later when he wants to make love. A man may be able to compartmentalize his feelings, but a woman is seldom able to do so. She needs foreplay throughout the day, long before they ever reach the bedroom. A woman needs to hear that he thinks of her during the day and how glad he is to be married to her. She needs to remind him of the long drive they took in the country last weekend or that lovely dinner they enjoyed together in that little French bistro. She needs to tell him how exciting she found it when he called to tell her that he could hardly wait to take her in his arms and make indecent proposals to her later that evening.

WHERE ARE THE FIREWORKS?

For sex to be good, it needs to be exciting. Women often accuse men of measuring their sexual ability by penile inches or the number of orgasms they can give their partners. Simultaneous orgasms or an orgasm every time rates right there at the top for most men. When a partner is concentrating on achievement, rather than on love, it is not at all difficult to understand why sex can become so boring.

As the saying goes, "The journey should be as important as, or more important than, the destination."

When Harriet first entered therapy, it was with great trepidation. She and her husband, Paul, had been together for twenty years. Both were very capable teachers in the local high school. Harriet was concerned her marriage had become so stagnant that it was impossible for any real emotional response to occur. Her sex life had become a great disappointment to her. She wanted to know how to get some sparks to fly.

"We spent the first years of our marriage learning how to become more efficient so that we could accomplish more. What we have succeeded in accomplishing is an organized, effective, sterile marriage. It is not fun. It's not even interesting. We fill each other's physical needs with expert technique. But I am left wondering, Is that all there is?

"Paul teaches history. It is a profession for which he was born. He devours books on the Native Americans, which is his great obsession. I teach English literature. Although reading is my grand passion, I find reading essays written by high school juniors usually less than intellectually stimulating. We have two girls. Elizabeth is in the tenth grade and Barbara is a freshman in college. I suppose I could describe our home as immaculate. Even though it is filled with books, there are seldom any out of place. Paul places every book in the book case, with the proper name plate, in alphabetical order. I must confess, I am just as bad. My spice shelf is arranged alphabetically, too. We live in a large apartment, near the school. We had no money for a down payment on a house when we were first married. Then, the children came along. We were always so comfortable in the apartment. The thought of taking on a mortgage, or re-alphabetizing all those books after we moved, was more than either of us could bear.

"I never thought much about sex before. Isn't that funny? Here I am, forty-six years old on my next birthday, and suddenly, all I think about is wanting Paul to make passionate love to me. We do have intercourse every Sunday afternoon, after church. The girls are usually away then and the apartment is quiet. They know we always take a nap on Sunday afternoons. They are thoughtful and try not to bother us. Last Sunday, when Paul began to pull down the spread, the neat, careful way he did it made me want to scream. I wanted him to toss the pillows on the floor, grab me, caress my breasts, and cover my face and body with kisses. But Paul was his usual, sweet, gentle self. This was what he was like when I married him. What is wrong with me? Why do I think, oh well, it's just ten minutes out of the day. It all seems so devastatingly boring to me.

"When I was a child, I had unlimited energy as I suppose most children do. I thought that energy would always be with me. Even after the children came, I still got out of bed at 6:00 a.m. every morning. Many mornings Paul would beg me to stay for a little sunrise sex, but I'd seldom give in. I knew if I didn't shower and dress before the children, I would be behind the rest of the day. I usually set the dinner table after I did the breakfast dishes. One Christmas Paul gave me a crock pot. I make most of my dinners in it. That way, the food can cook all day and dinner is never late, even if I am. It is universally misunderstood that teachers work only half days for nine months of the year. There are always meetings with the parents, professional workshops, and mountains of paperwork. Grading is one of my least enjoyable activities. But, all in all, I do love what I do and plan to continue until I am old enough to retire.

"Because of our demanding schedules, Paul and I have little time together. Elizabeth still lives at home. We are very careful to see that she is home by 10:00 p.m., does her homework, and does not monopolize the telephone. We are careful of what we discuss in our home. Sexy books and erotic material have no place there. I suppose you could say we are very strict parents, but then, we are rigid with our own desires as well. There is a place for everything, and everything is in its place. Isn't that how that old saying goes?"

What Harriet was *not* saying was that she wanted sex *not* in the same old place, or in the same old way. She wanted to feel free. She wanted to feel creative. She wanted to *feel*. She was sick of restrictive sexual encounters and her rigid lifestyle. Harriet was going through a mid-life crisis.

MID-LIFE MADNESS

When couples reach their forties and fifties, most of them become aware of their own mortality. They begin to realize that their lives are half over. They ruminate on what they have accomplished. They contemplate new horizons. Mid-life is a time to reflect on the fulfillment of hidden desires. For some, a deep dissatisfaction arises with personal relationships. A partner may want to be with someone who is more interesting, more exciting, someone who promises to provide the sexual stimulation felt to have been denied.

Although one of Paul and Harriet's daughters was still at home, Harriet was aware the time was nearing when she, too, would go away to school. Even though Harriet had always had a career, much of her life was focused around being a mother and homemaker. Letting go will be a very difficult process for Harriet. She will need to come to some sort of understanding of the meaning and direction her life will now take.

Because almost all of Harriet's care and attention had been spent on teaching and raising her family, very little energy had been invested in creating a rewarding, romantic sex life with her partner. What had brought her to therapy was the sudden realization and joy that someone was interested in her. Not her husband, but a male colleague at the school.

> "This is almost too embarrassing to tell. Last fall a new teacher joined my department. He instructs the gifted students in creative writing. Thomas and I spend almost all of our free time together discussing literature. He reads extensively and so do I. Thomas brings me the book section of the *New York Times* every Monday morning. We discuss the reviews over our lunch or on our coffee breaks. He thinks some of my observations are quite insightful.
>
> "I look forward to these conversations. I like other things about our meetings as well. Thomas notices little things. I changed my hairstyle last month from a chignon to wearing it loose, down to my shoulders, even though my hair is gray. Thomas likes the naturalness of it. Thomas says I am a woman who is aging within an aura of youth. He told me how he admires the way I walk proudly, with my head up and my shoulders straight. Thomas feels that a woman should look as young when she is walking away from you as she does when she is walking toward you. He says I maintain my youthfulness by my attitude. He appreciates women of depth. Thomas feels such women are intriguing and ageless."

Harriet said all of this in a hushed voice with the color in her cheeks rising perceptibly. Her manner had drastically changed from the way it had been when she was berating her predictable sex life with Paul. It is not uncommon for any woman to feel flushed with anticipation and ardor when she thinks or speaks about a man who has made her feel so special.

When sex is typically perfunctory and unsatisfying, partners will often grow resentful. In Harriet and Paul's marriage, so little time was spent in tender, caring, teasing conversation before going to bed that Harriet felt cheated. She wanted her mate's attention. Their sexual encounters were so brief, there was little time for any satisfying emotional response. A couple needs to have an *emotional connection* or their relationship will certainly deteriorate.

MAKING YOUR OWN HISTORY

What attracted Harriet to Thomas was the interest and sensitivity he expressed toward her. It is clear that she wishes these same tender, titillating emotions would be conveyed to her by her husband. It is not too late. When Paul returns home in the evenings, Harriet could interject some playfulness and teasing into their conversation. First, she could lose the crockpot. These appliances can be helpful once in a while, but little individuality or special care goes into a dinner cooked this way. Harriet could surprise Paul with his favorite foods which she probably hasn't prepared in years. That alone would get his attention.

After she has captured his interest by showing Paul this special consideration, she could then let the child in her emerge. By her own admission, she has lots of energy, when it is not sapped by boredom. Harriet needs to translate that energy into relearning how to be sexual. She had begun by changing her hair to a softer and more feminine style. Now Harriet could ask Paul to tell her frankly what he would find sexually appealing. Harriet needs to listen carefully to what Paul says without making any demands or criticisms. Her sudden interest in his desires might seem threatening to Paul at first. As Harriet pursues her sexual questioning, she should be careful and take her time. She cannot expect to relearn what makes Paul happy all in one conversation. Her questions could include such specifics as which positions he prefers and what erogenous zones are most stimulating to him. He will probably be puzzled by these questions, but eventually, he will most likely be flattered by her interest and care.

Although it is true that Paul was not making sexual overtures, it is also true that neither was Harriet. Both had compartmentalized sex into an hour's nap on Sunday afternoons. Harriet could end this constricting habit by giving broad sexual cues during the week. Their daughter was absent from the apartment on many evenings. This time would be ideal for doing something *together*, not separately.

Harriet could also give Paul the pleasant surprise of leisurely making love to *him*, while intently pleasing *herself*. This is not to suggest the total responsibility for sex should always fall on Harriet, but she does need to capture his attention to get things rolling. If she makes Paul feel that she is reacting to his potency, her satisfaction will create an intimate aphrodisiac to which Paul will certainly respond.

One of the things that Harriet found delightful about Thomas was his eagerness to discuss an interest they both shared. Harriet and Paul need to find a new interest that *they* can share. Harriet could suggest they learn the stories of operas from librettos she could borrow from the library or purchase in a bookstore. This would be a wonderful shared interest. Both love to read, and Paul, in particular, enjoys history. They might listen to favorite operas together in their apartment. For a memorable sexual interlude, Harriet and Paul could begin foreplay during the overture, then initiate erotic lovemaking during the second act. The finale of the opera would be a perfect background for the afterglow! Perhaps they could see some of their favorite operas performed, either in local productions or when they vacation. While watching the production, each partner would be able to visualize just what he or she was doing during the second act. What an intimate sexual experience they could share . . . .

USE IT OR LOSE IT

It is important for every woman to comprehend that a man may experience real fear about his ability to gain and sustain an erection. Most women understand that a man's ego is connected to his sexual prowess, but few realize how significant this can be to a man's self-esteem. Sexual ability and confidence are linked together for a man in the same way sex and love are intertwined for a woman. When a man wants to make love to his mate, but is unable to get an erection, he feels frustrated and humiliated. And, more importantly, he feels vulnerable. Usually he will try to hide these fears, but something in the relationship is always affected.

When a man begins to experience difficulty with erections, he will do almost anything to either avoid sex entirely or to complete sexual intercourse as fast as possible. Either technique can be very frustrating to his partner. While it is true, one cannot attribute all of a mate's behavior to performance anxiety, when a partner begins finding excuses not to have sex, this could certainly be the reason.

"Alex complained about how rotten his day had been as he came through the kitchen door. I concentrated on being busy at the stove, but I could not help but think to myself, Oh no, not again.

"The next words out of Alex's mouth were, 'What's for dinner?' as he tossed his jacket onto the family room couch and began undoing his tie.

"I had sent the two boys to my mother's so that we could have an evening alone together. We hadn't had a break in months. Alex recently joined a new engineering firm. Jobs are tight. He was laid off his last job after being with them for seven years. We really didn't expect the cutback would affect Alex, because he had been there so long. But, the firm's downsizing was severe. Alex applied at every engineering firm in the city, but it was seven months before he got this position. He works late most evenings and goes in even on Saturdays. Since we hadn't had sex in so long, I thought I would surprise him with this evening alone. I had made his favorite dinner. Alex loves roasted duckling with a mandarin orange sauce. I almost never make it. It takes too long and is expensive. Besides, the boys won't eat it. I knew he would be surprised. I set the table with candles and our good china on our screened-in back porch. It was lovely outside. I was just finishing the fresh peas when Alex came home so disgruntled.

"At first, I didn't let his tone bother me. After all, he wasn't expecting this special treat. I gave him time to wash his hands and notice that the kitchen table was not set and the boys were not around. He didn't notice. He poured himself a large scotch from the liquor cabinet in the family room and proceeded to go up for a shower before dinner. Oh well, I thought. I would give him time to freshen up and then maybe he would feel better. Twenty minutes passed. I couldn't keep the duck much longer. When I went into our bedroom to see what was keeping him, I found Alex sound asleep on the bed. I was furious. I didn't care that he was exhausted. I was tired too, and disappointed. I had spent the entire day in preparation for this terrific evening I had planned and he had fallen asleep. I shook Alex as hard as I could. He awakened startled. His first words were to ask if the boys were all right? I wanted him to ask if I was all right. My entire life was spent taking care of the children and Alex. When was someone going to take care of me?"

Cassy and Alex had a huge fight. The duck burned and the candles scorched her best tablecloth. The boys returned the next morning. No sexual liaison had occurred. Cassy sought counseling.

WHAT'S HAPPENING HERE?

For the first several months, Cassy was able to be very understanding about Alex's lack of interest in sex. She understood the loss of his job had created deep feelings of inadequacy in Alex. Most men equate their ability in the workplace with their machismo in the bedroom. When a woman is aware her mate is under severe stress, it is helpful to not place sexual pressure on her partner. Without realizing it, this is exactly what Cassy did. She had been thoughtful and considerate, but like most people, she has a breaking point. Cassy needs to know that when she's frustrated to the point of hysteria, there are certain options short of violence she can employ.

When a man complains he has a headache or just wants to nap or watch TV, he may be afraid he is not capable of making love. If Cassy were to suggest this, of course, Alex would deny it. In his eyes he has already suffered one failure. He has failed to keep a job at which he worked very diligently and felt very capable. He could not admit his frustration to himself and certainly not to Cassy. She needs to rebuild Alex's confidence. She could look at this as a challenge. If Cassy has a good imagination, she could play mistress to Alex. What is the definition of a mistress? Not being better at sex, not even necessarily looking sexy. Studies show that when men have affairs, the major reason is that the "other woman" *made them feel like they were someone very special.*

Cassy needs to help rebuild Alex's self-esteem. She could tell him that he is an excellent, caring father, and a wonderful lover. She could say how much she misses him in bed. It would not hurt to be more specific and describe to him in detail what he did in bed that makes her miss him the most. This is the time to be graphic. Describing to a mate the sexual acts that create the deepest arousal in his lover will turn him on. Because sexual avoidance can become a habit, it is important that Cassy not let too much time elapse before she initiates sex. This is one habit couples definitely want to break.

When sex begins to feel like a scheduled event without passion, intrigue, or romance, partners lose interest. For many couples, not having enough information about alternative sexual tools and methods keeps relationships from being fun. New positions, sexual toys, and various locations can all add up to more exciting sex. But the easiest, most effective way for partners to spice up their sex life is to vary the amount of time they spend making love. Sometimes quick can be great. At other times, a more leisurely style is more satisfying. The simple fact that lovemaking can vary in time and place can relieve monotony and add that spontaneous quality which results in orgasm and feelings of love and well being. So throw away the egg timer and indulge in a little sexual play, no matter how long it lasts.

CHAPTER 9

The Sexual Sahara

In this age of super moms, super dads, and super couples, there exists an equally unrealistic expectation that partners be super sexed. Couples need to be aware that the "Sexual Sahara," or, sexual dry spells, occur in the sex lives of almost every intimate relationship. There are several methods that help remedy these disappointing periods. It is not necessary for both partners to work at these solutions. Even if just one mate is able to take positive action, a sexual drought can be alleviated. Just remember, don't panic! Patience and planning are essential.

There are many reasons why couples fall in love, but the response to those feelings is almost universally the same. When love is new, it all seems so natural and easy. Your lover's faults are overlooked or thought to be charming. Hours are spent discussing and sharing every intimate thought and desire. Couples trust each other completely. A spouse feels certain that this wonderful adoring person who has come into his or her life and changed it so magically would never do anything to destroy that perfect trust. Seldom do partners contemplate the changes that will occur as they mature. Although many professionals claim that all relationships become comfortable rather than passionate after a while, it is possible for a relationship to remain fulfilling and exciting. It is possible, but it requires lots of work.

A teary-eyed Gloria related the details of her marriage to Tony.

"We have been married for eight years. We have a lovely new home and three wonderful little girls. I'm an interior designer, and Tony is an architect. When we met, I was managing the showroom of one of leading interior design studios in town. I loved that job and I got to be rather good at it. One day this gorgeous guy, rather on the small side but very well-built, came into the studio and asked for me. I was sitting at the massive desk where clients would sign in, and so I put out my hand and introduced myself.

"'I am Gloria,' I responded. 'How can I help you?' I prayed he wouldn't notice that my hand was shaking when we touched. He was very different from the men who usually entered the design studio. His rugged sunburned look even in winter was very appealing to me. When he introduced himself, I immediately recognized his name. He was the outstanding architect I had been reading about recently. He was getting a lot of exposure in the press. Then, I really was puzzled. What was he doing here?

"Tony explained that he was building this new home for himself. Several of the interior designers he knew had told him about me. They had described my avant-garde taste and creativity. Tony wanted to know if he could hire me on a free-lance basis to decorate his new home.

"'But, what about your wife?' I asked, dreading his answer.

"Tony responded quite honestly. 'Oh, I'm not married. That is why I was hoping you will help me. It is an immense home. I have neither the patience nor the talent to decorate this house. You could choose your own schedule. I will pay you well.'

"I would have taken the job for nothing! I was twenty-eight at the time. I had fantasized for years about some wonderful prince charming sweeping me off my feet. I never dreamed that handsome prince would actually find me where I worked. The next seven months were exhilarating ones for me. I worked at the design studio from 9:00 a.m. until 5:00 p.m. Now the days really flew. I could not wait until 5:00 p.m. when I was out of the door like a flash, into my little blue sports car, and on the freeway to meet at Tony's new home. It was a smashing place. All angles and glass. The walls of the house were not square, as they are in most homes. They were hexagon shaped. That presented a real decorating challenge for me. I rose to the occasion. The couches and chairs, lamps, desk, and tables I had selected were massive, modern, and regal. The wall coverings and carpets were dramatic but tasteful. I had developed an intriguing look within a personal ambiance by utilizing mementos of Tony's throughout the house. This home would certainly be the most sumptuous I had ever decorated. The success of this job could send me lots of new clients. I was already contemplating the raise I would receive from my employer.

"Because we were together almost every evening, Tony began taking me to dinner after our meetings. He chose wonderful little bistros, most of which I had never been to before. I began dressing better. I didn't want to embarrass him by looking like a shop girl. Now I had places to wear the clothing I had always wanted. My wardrobe was simple, but sophisticated. Tony would murmur his approval when I appeared wearing something new. He was also very pleased at how the house was taking shape. I thought it was a shame he was going to live there alone, but I didn't have the nerve to say so.

"After eight months of dating, Tony called and asked me to meet him at the park near his new home. Puzzled, I agreed. I couldn't help but worry that something might be wrong. When I arrived and parked my car next to his, I saw Tony had a picnic basket and a bottle of wine in the backseat. It was autumn. The leaves were falling. It was just beautiful in the late afternoon sun. We took a walk along one of the trails. Suddenly, Tony turned around, looked at me very seriously, and asked me if I would like to be married at Christmastime. It was fortunate he was holding on to me, because I could have fallen into the ravine. Of course, I responded 'Yes,' and we were married on Christmas Eve.

"I thought our marriage was very successful, until recently. Tony adores the girls and is an excellent father. I pride myself on keeping my figure. I am very busy working as a designer while the girls are in school. We have just built another new home that I decorated. We are able to take wonderful vacations. This last spring, Tony took me to Paris. Then, the other evening, Tony shocked me by saying he didn't know if he loved me anymore. I know our sex life isn't as exciting as it used to be, but I love Tony very much. He says he loves me, but he is not *in love* with me."

FALLING IN LOVE WITH LOVE

When a couple is first together, they feel the romance will last forever. No one ever imagines that one could fall out of love. When a partner suggests he or she no longer feels the same, a mate may believe that it is the lover who has changed. A woman will say that he is so different now. A man will say that she has changed. Rarely do people consider what has changed about themselves.

After a woman has absorbed the hurt, she usually concludes that there is something wrong with her. What has she done wrong? A woman will change her hair, her makeup, her behavior in order to recapture a mate's love. When that doesn't work, she gets angry. Gloria was no different. She thought Tony's feelings had changed because they were not having sex as often as when they first met. When sexual problems occur, it is usually only a symptom of other problems in the marriage.

"I know I haven't been spending much time doing things with Tony lately. He was disappointed when I missed the opening of his new housing development. His company built some gorgeous new condos down by the lake.

"We have a favorite television program on Wednesday evenings we used to watch after the children were in bed. Now that I am working, I usually have paperwork and phone calls to make in the evenings. I try to watch but I am too busy.

"Tony loves to read. He finds it comforting when we settle down with a good book together in the family room. He often reads aloud paragraphs from the books that he feels I would find interesting. I do the same with a particularly enjoyable portion of the books I read, too. I enjoy this time together just as much as he does. But by the time I get the children in bed, take a leisurely bath to get the tension of the day out, and make a few calls, I am too tired to read.

"We used to belong to a photography club that met twice a month. Tony bought me some expensive equipment for my birthday and taught me how to use it. We took classes together to learn how to develop our own color shots. Tony put a darkroom in our new house. The photos I took of the girls came out so well we have them hanging in the family room. As much as I enjoyed these classes, I really don't have time for them right now. Tony still goes, but when he nudges me, I really feel he doesn't understand I have different priorities in my life.

"The competition among interior designers is fierce. I need to get re-established. When we returned from Paris, I was so far behind with my clients I thought I'd never catch up. I also missed the girls terribly while we were away. I usually spend weekends taking them to museums and movies so they won't feel neglected. My life is so full and so busy, I guess I forgot to be sensitive to Tony's needs. But, he always seems so self-assured and understanding. If he was unhappy, he didn't show it. How could he hurt me this way?"

It was clear the close emotional ties that kept Tony and Gloria sexually connected had eroded. A great deal of work was required. Gloria needs to ask Tony some very difficult questions. She need not expect an answer. He may not know the answers. Her questioning should be the impetus for Tony to think about the issues she has raised. These need to be questions to work on that may take days, or months, or years. Even though Tony had told Gloria he was no longer *in love* with her, this does not mean this marriage is over. Tony is trying to get Gloria's attention. What he is really saying is that he is feeling discontented. Gloria needs to find out why. She needs to ask him what the reasons are, even though some are not difficult to see. Tony probably has been giving Gloria signals for quite some time with vague hints and complaints, but she has not noticed. When he told Gloria that he was falling out of love with her, Tony certainly got her attention.

Gloria spoke in great detail about returning to the work she loved while her children were in school. Almost all of her energy was absorbed in reviving her career. The people she met who became her friends and confidants were not shared by Tony. Gloria had created a new life for herself, away from her family. Gloria needs to ask herself if by making this decision, perhaps she, too, was feeling discontented. By concentrating almost exclusively on her career, was she creating a new life that did not include Tony?

Gloria needs to reevaluate her priorities. This does not necessarily mean relinquishing her career, but simply scheduling her time in a more productive way. She needs to make Tony realize that just as she was the most important thing in his life, he was the most important thing in hers. This couple needs to negotiate. After Gloria gives Tony the opportunity to verbalize his complaints, it is important for her not to retaliate by asking him to leave. Tony should not ask Gloria to change within a certain length of time. These demands are responses mates often use to protect their hurt feelings and to gain control over a frightening situation. They need to listen to each other carefully and begin to renegotiate their lives, while respecting each other's needs. Intimate relationships require constant negotiation over the years. When a couple is able to communicate unhappiness and work out problems successfully, sexual dry spells that could result in permanent separation can be alleviated.

What is the secret of staying in love? Shared intimacy. Partners need to feel they are the most important reason for each other's being. One definition of being "in love" is the feeling of being the center of each other's life. Of course, this does not mean that partners do not have individual interests that are not shared. What it does mean is that it is important for couples to maintain an intimate connection.

PROMISES, PROMISES

When Kim, fifty-two and stunning, came to therapy, it was because of her fear of losing Gil. They had been living together for several months. Now, Kim's feelings of anger toward Gil seemed overwhelming to her. She was afraid if she confronted him with the issues that were bothering her, she would lose him forever and be alone for the rest of her life. This was a risk Kim was not willing to take.

"Gil and I have been living together in my house for about seven months. This was the house I had lived in with my former husband before our divorce ten years ago. I am a travel agent and Gil works for a cruise line. We met at a company party that was very loud and crowded. No one asked me to dance. I am an excellent dancer and like to show off my intricate footwork. Most of the people at this party were about my age.

"One of the reasons I like to go to these affairs is that it gives me an opportunity to meet new men. I don't go for the bar scene. The woman seem so aggressive. Most of the singles are younger than I. As I grow older, it seems to become more difficult to attract available men.

"I was contemplating leaving when a gorgeous guy approached me. He was about my age, maybe even a little younger. He was snapping his fingers as he asked me to dance. What great rhythm. We spent the rest of the evening together and ended up back at my place where he spent the night.

"Gil takes lots of cruises. I guess that makes sense, since he works for a cruise line. I know he meets lots of women on these trips. He wasn't shy about sharing this information with me. He is an excellent dancer. We share a few other interests as well. We both like to golf. Las Vegas is a favorite vacation spot for us both. We enjoy gambling a little. Actually, Gil enjoys gambling a lot. But, I didn't know this when we first began living together. Gil is a skillful and sensitive lover. He knows just where to touch me. I have multiple orgasms with him, something I never had with my ex-husband.

"We began seeing each other almost every night when Gil was not traveling. One evening, we were sitting in this little bar we both like, when Gil complained about all the rent he was paying for his condo when he actually spent so little time there. I picked up on his cue immediately. I suggested he move into my home and we split the expenses. He jumped at the opportunity. His decision made me feel fantastic. I hated living alone. But, in ten years I had not met anyone I thought I would like to be with on a permanent basis. Gil said he was handy around the house and that he wanted to put in a vegetable garden in my backyard. That would save us some money on the grocery bill. It seemed like the perfect arrangement.

"In the seven months we have lived together, Gil has yet to fix a thing around the house. When my faucet was leaking last month, I had to call a plumber. Oh, he promises to do things. It's just that he never finds the time. He will always get to it after he finishes whatever else he is doing. But by then it's too late, or he forgets. The garden he spent so much time planning is non-existent. I threw the last of the seed catalogs in the garbage weeks ago. It is true that he has a bad back. What upsets me is, Why did he suggest putting in a garden in the first place?

"About six weeks ago, Gil and I went to Vegas for a long weekend. We had talked about it for months and he made the reservations. I bought a sexy low-cut jumpsuit and some wicked-looking black lingerie. We hadn't been making love as frequently as we had in the past. Gil said he had a lot on his mind, and my sex drive wasn't as demanding as it used to be. I thought the atmosphere of Las Vegas would revitalize our sex life.

"When we arrived, the hotel had mixed up our reservations. No room was ready, but they promised we would have one in three hours. I was disappointed. I wanted to change into my new outfit. Being a good sport, I didn't say anything. We headed for the blackjack tables. Within the first hour Gil had lost all the money he had brought with him. He asked to borrow money from me. I was furious. I had saved about nine hundred dollars for gambling and maybe a special gift to myself from one of the fabulous stores in the hotel. When Gil remarked there would be no point in staying if we couldn't gamble, I relented. After all, he said he would pay me back. His losing streak couldn't go on the entire four days. I would be helping him to regain his losses. I didn't need anything new to wear, anyway. Although I was angry, I said nothing and gave him the travelers checks.

"Gil's winning streak never materialized. I had to charge our hotel bill and our dinners on my Mastercard. This was one time I wised they only took Visa. We never danced, never made love. We never even saw a show. In fact, I never saw Gil, unless I stood next to him at the blackjack table. Even after he lost all my money, he enjoyed standing for hours and watching the other players. As angry as I was, I said nothing. I didn't want Gil to think I was cold-hearted, besides, I wasn't certain I had a right to be angry. I might disapprove of how Gil behaved, but getting angry about it wouldn't change anything.

"The last straw came yesterday, when I opened the mail. Usually Gil gets home before I do but he was away on business. He always puts the letters and bills in a flowered china letter holder I bought in Bermuda years ago. Imagine my shock when I found a disconnect notice for the electricity. Our bill had not been paid in months! The utilities were Gil's responsibility. I never questioned he was not fulfilling his end of our bargain.

"I was furious. When he returned from his trip that evening, I couldn't bring myself to make love. When he approached me, I pulled away. When he asked me what was wrong, I told him 'nothing.' He was very upset and told me he should have stayed in Miami, where the women are much more sexually available than I had been recently. I am afraid that if I show my anger he will feel threatened and leave me."

LISTEN TO YOUR ANGER

Angry feelings are worth listening to. Anger is a signal your body sends, saying that feelings are hurt, rights are being violated, or needs are not being met. Angry feelings can signal when a mate is not addressing important issues. Perhaps values, desires, or ambitions are being compromised in the relationship. Anger can signify that one partner is doing too much, at the expense of personal growth of another. The pain of personal anger can motivate rejection of a partner's demands and expectations.

When anger is allowed to fester, it can inhibit sexual feeling. Many sexual dry spells occur because a mate is withholding physical love instead of expressing anger. But when partners are able to work through that anger, it allows the couple the freedom to say "yes" to the desires of the inner self.

Women typically are more hesitant to express anger than men. Most women are taught since childhood to be good little girls. They are conditioned to smile and deny negative feelings. A woman will ask herself if her anger is legitimate, if she has the right to be angry. As much as she may dislike the disapproval she receives when she expresses her angry feelings, her anger signals the necessity for change.

Although Kim was a mature woman, she had not yet realized that anger is neither legitimate nor illegitimate. Everyone has the right to be angry. It is an emotion that needs to be recognized so that it does not block other feelings. Kim needs to tell Gil what was bothering her in a noncritical way. It is important for her not to antagonize him by saying, "You don't take care of your responsibilities. You expect me to provide financial support when you do not. You have not been honest with me." Although each of these statements may be true, her hostility might make it impossible for the two of them to discuss the problem rationally. Kim needs to tell Gill in a nonconfrontational manner that his behavior is unacceptable to her. This way, she is not criticizing *him* for doing something bad or good; she is simply acknowledging her own feelings. If Gil cares for Kim as much as she does for him, he might try to change his behavior with some professional help. If Gil feels he is unable to deal with Kim's anger and questions the validity of her feelings, perhaps she would be better off without him. Then she would be free to find a partner whom she could trust and who would give her the love and respect she deserves.

SEX ON THE HIGH WIRE

Krissy, an aerobics instructor, entered therapy for a very unusual reason. She and Eric had been married for three years and had been together for four and a half. All of their friends considered them the perfect couple. She always laughed at his silly jokes, even though she had heard them numerous times. They held hands in the movies. They danced with their eyes closed as though they were one person. They both seemed to express a surprised joy at being in each other's presence. They were delightful to be with and their social calendar was filled for months. Sex was frequent but, for Krissy, it was becoming a little boring.

"I can't believe I am complaining about this. Eric is a sexually attentive husband. I know I am lucky to have him. Yet, even though we are both willing to experiment with new positions, I'm finding I'm a little bit bored with the *trying*. Oh, sure, the sex is good, but it is not sensational. It seems contrived to me. Eric is forever suggesting something new. Because I am an aerobics instructor, I suppose he feels he can manipulate my body into any position. This seems to be a real turn-on for Eric. It was for me at first too. Now I feel like he is making love to a mechanical object and not to me. I would give anything for the good, old-fashioned missionary position and a bouquet of flowers.

"On our vacation this past summer, we rented a houseboat and traveled to Canada through the Thousand Islands. It was very beautiful. Eric loved to drive the houseboat. I spent the days reading on the deck. In the evenings, we docked at wonderful little inns where we ate romantic dinners together. We met interesting people from Canada and the States.

"Being alone on the houseboat gave us a wonderful opportunity for creative sex. We used the upper bunk, the lower bunk, the head, and the luggage rack. We made love under the stars wondering who might be watching us through a telescope. Eric had decided not to shave on the trip. He said he wanted to look like a real sea captain when we returned from our vacation. I hadn't realized that also meant he wouldn't shower. There were public showers near the community laundry room that all the boaters shared when they docked. He complained he could not shower with all those strangers and that swimming in the river was good enough. Good enough for him, maybe, but not for me. One night, four days into the ten-day trip, I couldn't stand his body odor any longer. I took my lavender hand lotion and lathered his body with it while I caressed him. The aroma was so penetrating that I thought Eric would have to shower before we went to dine at the inn. I thought my frosting of his body was very funny. I could not stop my giggles. Eric completely ignored my playfully subtle message and proceeded to make love to me as though only my body were involved, not my feelings. He ignored my discomfort and avoided the public shower. He didn't get it.

"When we returned from our trip on the houseboat, one of our friends gave a party. Everyone was anxious to see the pictures of our unusual vacation. I was very upset when Eric passed photos of me topless, cupping my breasts, and leering into the camera like a voluptuous tramp. I felt our sex life was personal. I certainly didn't want our friends to share in our sexual play.

"We have created such an illusion of the perfect couple, but I no longer feel we are. I don't know how to tell Eric that I want him to be more sensitive to my needs. I am still upset about his showing of the photographs. My memories of the trip are far less enthusiastic than his. I haven't been able to make love to him in the same way since. I certainly don't want him looking for greener pastures. How can I revive my sexual feelings?"

Subtlety has its place, but Krissy was being too circumspect. She needs to tell Eric how sexy it makes her feel when he smells so fresh and clean after his shower. She needs to make him aware that a woman's sense of smell is often more sensitive than a man's. Although some men enjoy the aroma of a woman's body after strenuous exercise, most women cannot reciprocate the delight in a man's body odor.

OVERSEXED ANONYMOUS

Eric seems to be sexually self-indulgent. He is absorbed in his own pleasure. He pays little or no attention to his partner's needs as evidenced by his sharing of erotic photographs with friends. Eric is very goal-oriented in his desires and is unaware of his partner's needs. Krissy is left feeling unimportant and unloved. She is trying to stifle her anger at feeling used. Although he may love her dearly, Eric is showing all the symptoms of the sexual performer. He appears passionate and hot, yet Krissy can sense that something is not quite right.

Krissy needs to reassure Eric that she loves him for himself, not just for his performance in bed. She needs to encourage him to *feel* that love. With great sensitivity, Krissy needs to convey that she wishes Eric would make love to her in a way that is not contrived, but just simply *with* her.

Although Eric prided himself on his creative approach to sex, Krissy resents being treated like a human pretzel. She wants Eric to cherish her as a special human being. She does not want to be regarded as a gymnast training for the next Olympics. Krissy craves the romance that she needs in order for her to feel *in love* with Eric. One of the most effective ways for Krissy to create this aura of romance is for her to become the seducer. Krissy needs to initiate sex. Although most men dream of seduction by their mate as the ultimate sexual fantasy, it is often difficult for a man to enjoy this reversal of roles. Krissy needs to alert Eric to her sexual advances. If he is taken by surprise, Eric may not be able to respond. His erection might be elusive. She needs to proceed carefully, remembering that it was Eric who always initiated sex when he felt he was ready. If Krissy is to take the initiative, she should tantalize Eric with extended foreplay so that he will be excited and erect. If Krissy treats Eric the way she wants to be treated and is very loving in her approach, she may find old-fashioned love can even be improved upon.

CHAPTER 10

Pillow Talk

Experts almost universally agree that the key to solving most relationship problems is improved communication. Although partners may frequently talk about sex, few really understand what the other is saying. Even fewer feel comfortable in expressing their wants and needs in a way that is not hurtful or destructive. Partners need specific tools in order to break negative communication patterns and to establish positive ones. Communication is an art form all couples can develop in order to relate to one another more effectively.

Before mates are able to communicate effectively, there must be implicit trust between them. They need to feel certain that they will be listened to with great sensitivity, that their feelings will be placed above all else. Even when trust is firmly established between partners, it still may be very difficult for some to understand what a lover's words actually mean. Sometimes a partner may say one thing, but the other hears something else entirely. This can happen when a partner is trying to speak with great tact, because the words he or she chooses are indirect and confusing. At other times, partners may dismiss each other's statements as frivolous or impossible because a mate does not comprehend what the other is saying.

When couples are unable to communicate effectively with one another, they often feel angry and upset. These strong emotions negate feelings of love and the intimate connection that all couples wish to have. Partners may find it difficult to tap into feelings of love for each other. To avoid this problem, partners must take ownership of their feelings and express them. If a mate is unable to express these emotions, the conflict can never be fully resolved. Feelings of love can be numbed by layers and layers of tension that have not been released. Most partners are afraid to *fully* express emotion to a mate. Often a mate may dare to tell a partner only a portion of what is felt because of the fear of further rejection or retaliation. When only a portion of the truth is relayed to a partner, the remainder prevents honest communication between lovers.

Take the case of Laurie and Jim, a middle-age couple who had been together for nearly thirty years. Their otherwise happy marriage had come to a standstill when they stopped being completely honest and open with each other. "I was elated when the college called and informed me I had the job. Assistant dean of Student Affairs for our local community college! Imagine. I had just completed my doctorate, after many years of hard work." Laurie beamed with pleasure as she spoke. She was obviously very proud of her achievements.

"It was difficult to earn an advanced degree while I was raising a family. There are so many responsibilities—car pools and parent teacher meetings to attend. I carried more guilt during that period of my life than anyone can possibly imagine. My children would complain that all the other mothers had time to bake cookies and take them to the mall. I never would have gotten through it, except for the loving support of my husband, Jim. That is why it is so unbelievable that I am here now because of my problems with my husband.

"Jim was so proud of my educational achievements. You see, we met over thirty years ago in college when I was a freshman and he was a senior. Jim was class president and an honors student. I was a silly little girl with curly hair who loved a good time. I was so busy with parties and social events, it was two months before Jim could finally take me out on a date. We went for a drive in the country in his funny old Ford and ended up back at the campus pizza palace where our table was swarmed by boys who teased me and made Jim furious.

"Jim was so different than anyone I had ever dated. He was very serious. Instead of the next football game, his conversation focused around how important it was for a young couple to buy a house and not spend all their money on rent. Couple! Marriage! House! All I was thinking about was a career in fashion and a year in Europe.

"Jim proposed at least five times before I finally accepted. Some of my friends were already 'pinned,' which was what the period before engagement was called in those years for members of Greek societies. After a couple exchanged fraternity and sorority pins, there was a tradition called a 'serenade.' Sorority sisters would stand outside on the porch dressed in white blouses and black skirts while the 'pinned' girl was presented with a bouquet of red roses. The couple was then serenaded with favorite love songs by a group of his fraternity brothers. Looking back, it all seems very corny, but when I was eighteen, it was a thrilling experience. I felt then that all my life I would bask in those heady feelings of love. I thought I had the best of both worlds: Sorority sisters who would be lifelong friends and a handsome fraternity man who adored me and would take care of me. What a fantasy, though I did not know it then.

"We married with all our friends in attendance. Jim served his two years in the service and returned to find me typing in an insurance office and living for the day I could become pregnant and quit. We bought a small home, and the first of our three children was born. I really loved being a mother. There was no game I did not play, no cookie I did not bake. When Jennifer and Sally entered school and Kevin was in kindergarten, I thought, What will I do now? They only need me from three in the afternoon until bedtime. Bored by bridge and lunch with my friends, I enrolled at the local university to earn the degree I had so happily discarded so many years before.

"Jim was wonderfully supportive. He liked the idea that, unlike the wives of his friends, I had serious interests. Jim was earning enough money and said he felt grateful that he could now give me what I had given up so willingly for him.

"After I received my undergraduate diploma, it seemed only natural to go on for an advanced degree. I loved the classes. I met so many interesting people. Jim relished the stories I shared late at night when we were in bed. Our sex life was wonderful then. We were like two highly charged firecrackers coming together in one spontaneous explosion.

"Once I graduated, I was faced with the decision of what I would do with all this education. Jobs were scarce and I really didn't know what I wanted. One of my instructors at the university told me there was an opening for the position of assistant dean of Student Affairs at our community college. It's an administrative position but I thought I would enjoy it more than teaching. When I got the job, that is when my marital problems began.

"Jim was very angry when I told him I had accepted the job. I thought he would be happy for me. I was truly shocked with his response. What had he expected? He had always been there for me during those difficult years of studying. Now that I had completed my education, didn't he think I was going to work?

"What Jim told me, after my first explosion, was that he expected that now we would travel. Our children live in different states. He had it all planned. Christmas with one daughter, Easter with the other, and Thanksgiving with our son and his family. All the children and grandchildren would come to be with us at whatever home we were visiting at the time. Jim said he was contemplating an early retirement. News to me! And, after all these years, we could spend our time enjoying each other with no responsibilities. I stopped exploding. I began to cry.

"Our sex life, which had been so inventive and spontaneous throughout our marriage, literally stopped. Jim would either be in bed and supposedly asleep when I got out of the shower, or claimed he had a headache. This week he is catching a cold. I don't understand his complete withdrawal from me sexually. I can't get him to talk about it. I miss him in bed, but I am angry at him, too. Even though I am nearly fifty, I find I want sex more than ever. Other men still seem to find me attractive. Why doesn't Jim?"

WHEN THE ROLE OF PROVIDER IS THREATENED

Very often in a marriage, when roles change, a partner can feel threatened. Problems may arise that partners have difficulty resolving. A mate who has assumed the role of provider may have problems accepting a partner encroaching on his "territory." Whereas a woman may look forward to her new responsibility, a man may feel she is trying to undermine his authority.

Jim had enjoyed the years he had taken care of Laurie. Now she was entering a new arena where she would be independent and he did not have control. Laurie felt hurt and angry because Jim not only had made future plans without consulting her, but no longer seemed interested in having sex. Laurie needs to use her anger as a tool for change in their relationship. She needs to ask herself what the real issue is. What is there about the situation that makes her so angry? What does she feel? What does she want to accomplish?

Who is responsible for what? What, specifically, does Laurie want to change? What is she willing to do and what is she not?

Jim was very angry with Laurie because he felt he could not change or control her decision to become employed in a full-time job. Since he was unable to express his anger honestly and directly, he blocked his feelings which resulted in his thwarted sexual desire. This couple needs to invest that same energy now absorbed by anger into clarifying each partner's position and choice. Silent submission or ineffective fighting is not using communication in a positive way.

Laurie will not be able to change Jim if he does not want to change his feelings. Jim will not be able to change Laurie for the same reason. Partners must understand and be sympathetic to each other's needs in order for change to occur. This couple needs to re-invest their energy into working out their differences so they will not be trapped in endless cycles of fighting and blaming.

STATIC ON THE LINE

A couple may endlessly incorporate new sexual techniques, but if partners can't communicate what they *like* to one another, sex is never going to be wonderful and inspiring. Of course, only a few short years ago, it was not considered ladylike for a woman to express pleasure when her mate touched her in places that women of a former era might never have admitted they possessed. Back then, explicit description of *what* a lover liked and *where* she liked it was considered taboo. It is only in recent years that partners feel the freedom to graphically describe what feels good and what does not.

When Nina, an outgoing young woman, came to therapy, it was because she didn't feel comfortable with her new boyfriend's love-making technique. She suspected he was somewhat inexperienced with women, and she didn't know how to approach this highly sensitive issue.

"The first time Brent asked me out, I thought I would explode with pleasure. Or maybe it was just the anticipation of the pleasure I was sure he would give me after we got to know each other better. Brent is an investment broker in the same firm where I work.

"I just graduated from college a few months ago with a degree in communications. I had answered almost every ad in the classifieds. Everyone graduates in communications today. Jobs in radio and television are impossible to find. My folks said I had to support myself now since they had paid for four years of school, so I took the first job I was offered. Although my position as a receptionist doesn't pay well, it's fine for now.

"Well, anyway, here I am, working in this dreamy office, and this great looking guy asks me out. Brent is new there, too. In fact, he just moved to town and doesn't really know anyone yet. We talked a lot on my breaks. I brought him doughnuts for his coffee a few times. The other guys teased me that I had a crush on Brent but he thought it was sweet. I guess that's what made him ask me out in the first place. That was four months ago. We've been going hot and heavy ever since.

"I suppose you think it's strange that someone my age would see a sex therapist, but I've really got this problem. I had another boyfriend before Brent, named Steven, and sex with him was terrific. He was so *aware*! He knew all my hot spots. I could tell he had been around. No one could know all that from being with one partner. At the time it used to bother me that I was not his only lover. Now, I miss some of that expertise. When Brent makes love to me, it's like he really doesn't know what to do. I want to tell him, because I think I'm in love with him, but I don't want to scare him away."

It is not unusual for a man of any age to be unsure of how to make love to a woman. When a woman meets a good-looking man and has romantic feelings for him, it does not occur to her that he might know as little as she does about making love. Partners need to tell each other what feels good. They need to explore and communicate their desires to each other. It is this very sense of exploration and discovery that generates those sexual feelings of excitement. When everything is new and fresh, the anticipation acts as the motivation for sex. Lovemaking diminishes when partners no longer celebrate that feeling of expectation. Because women are preconditioned to acknowledge emotions, while men are taught from early childhood to conceal intimate feelings, it is usually the woman who is more aware of what she needs emotionally during lovemaking.

Even though today's woman is equal in all other aspects of life, she may still have difficulty with asking for what she wants in bed. She may not want to be considered as aggressive or demanding. Because women are so much better conditioned to handle emotional matters than most men, it becomes even more important for women to take the lead in sexual communication. There is a sexual language that can be learned to express desires from naughty to rapturous. This sexual conversation is subtle and caring but in order to be effective, it must be specific.

I DIDN'T MEAN *THAT*!

When a woman says, "I want you to make love to me in a different way tonight," her mate could be totally confused. Does she mean she wants oral sex or a vibrator or a third person in bed with them? Being nonspecific can be interpreted as scary or bossy by a lover. Nina wanted Brent to make love to her more assertively. If she were to say so in this way, he might feel everything he had been doing thus far had been wrong. Instead of being critical or sounding like a sex manual, Nina could say something like this to Brent. "I love the way you undress me. You're such a tease! When you so slowly stroke my body, your touch makes me tingle all over. I feel hot and deliciously sensual. I can hardly wait until we are in bed together. I wonder what it would feel like if you ripped my blouse off and began making love to me while I was still wearing my stockings and garter belt?" Or, "You have the greatest buns. I love to hold them. When I watch you move, it really turns me on. When we make love, where do you like to hold me?" Nina could ask Brent what he fantasizes about when he thinks of sex. Then, Nina might suggest they act out one or two fantasies together. Sharing a fantasy can often offer a great release to a timid sexual partner. Showing how much she cares about his needs will probably stimulate Nina as much as it will Brent.

Nina could use specific body language to reinforce her verbal message. She could take his hand gently and guide it to the parts of her body she would like to be stroked or touched more aggressively. When approaching orgasm, Nina could put her hand on a part of

Brent's body that he will find especially gratifying. Body language can also be used to express pleasure, such as stretching and purring while telling a partner how fantastic she feels with what he is doing. Nina needs to be very *specific*. When she compliments her lover, instead of using vague language to tell Brent he has a great body, Nina could tell him how she shamelessly wishes to cover every inch of his perfect body with her kisses. On the other hand, she should not give compliments that are not honest. Every man is aware when his gut is too large or his rib cage too pronounced. If Nina were to gush about something Brent knows is false, he would think she was being dishonest, whether she intended to be or not.

Nina might also find it helpful to pepper her sexual patter with humor and playfulness. Even an investment broker needs a little comic relief in his life. For instance, if Brent is fumbling around uncomfortably during lovemaking, Nina can introduce a little levity into the moment by telling him what she needs in her most outrageous Mae West imitation. Or, if the situation starts to feel too tense or pressured, she can initiate a "tickling war." In situations like these, technique is not the major issue. Partners need to relax and find pleasure in the searching and the sharing.

STOP THE WORLD AND LET ME GET OFF!

Mindy and Frank were the parents of two small children. Both partners were raised in a strict religious environment and continued these family traditions with their three-year-old twins. Mindy was a free-lance copy writer for an advertising agency. Frank was a private investigator for an insurance company. They were introduced by mutual friends at a rock concert six years before. Now they were settled in a small ranch home in a suburb inhabited by other young families. Weekends were spent at neighborhood barbecues, running errands, and washing cars. On Sundays, they usually visit with their respective parents and escort their twins to birthday parties. Mindy felt they were like most other young couples, making plans to move into a larger home and being fairly contented with their less-than-sensational love life.

"It is very difficult being a working mother. Although I work only twenty hours a week, with young children at home, it seems as though I am constantly busy. Perhaps 'overwhelmed' is a better word. My days are so full, I usually fall into bed, exhausted. I am working part-time in order to save my salary for a larger home. Frank says it won't be forever, but some days it feels like it.

"Three mornings a week I take our twins to a lovely woman in the neighborhood who baby-sits while I am at work. Before I pick them up, I try to grocery shop. It is just too difficult to shop with the twins. There is no room in the shopping cart for two toddlers. On the days I am not working in my office, I take the twins to the pediatrician or run all those other endless errands. As soon as we get home, after I give the children juice and some toys to play with in front of the television set, I start dinner. Frank helps me with the dishes.

"Even with disposable diapers, there is always laundry to do. I do most of my housecleaning on weekends, but there is always the mess of daily living to straighten up. I have to clean the bathrooms every day. We are attempting potty training. I feel we should be successful in about three years. I don't think I've ever heard of a child entering the first grade in diapers, although my two might be the first.

"I bathe the children and try to read them a story before bedtime. After they are asleep, there are toys to pick up, lunches to pack, and phone calls to return. Our folks do like to hear what our twins are doing, eating, and saying. They are concerned, and worry that we are too busy to be good parents. As well-meaning as our folks are, it is impossible for them to help us very often either financially or with baby-sitting. I am very well organized, but sometimes I think I'll never be able to do it all again the next day.

"The other evening, when we were in bed, Frank began stroking my breasts. This usually means he wants to make love. Then, he whispered in my ear that he wanted me to say something dirty to him. He asked me to describe what I wanted him to do to me in very explicit vulgar language. I was shocked! He had never requested such a thing of me before.

"I was puzzled as to why he wanted me to say these things to him in bed. Was he seeing someone else? Why was he asking me to behave in a way that was not natural for me? I can't say I was totally turned-off by Frank's request. It was just that I felt confused. I thought that what we were all about was family and expressing tender loving feelings toward each other. I need some help handling this new situation in our lives."

What a man often experiences after the birth of a child is that the mate who once ignited his sexual fires has become the responsible, conscientious, rule-orientated facsimile of his mother. Where once his partner was ready and eager for spontaneous, passionate lovemaking when they were alone, she now has no time and is exhausted fulfilling needs other than his. This image is definitely not a turn-on.

Of course, it is only natural that when a woman becomes a mother, she bonds with her child. Her child's needs become paramount, overshadowing those of her mate. Most of her thoughts and energy are centered around this new little person who was created through the partners' expression of love. As exciting as the prospect of fatherhood is for most men, it comes with the realization that now his mate's love must be shared. Jealousy is a feeling that is difficult for any man to admit. This is especially so when it involves his own child. But jealousy is a real emotion that needs to be dealt with. When Frank asked Mindy to verbalize her desires in specific vulgarities, he was attempting to help Mindy separate her maternal love for their children from the erotic feelings she had for him.

If Mindy felt too uncomfortable to express her love for Frank in this way, she did have other options. It is important for Mindy to understand that Frank's request was an effort to communicate his need for her to return as his erotic partner. When one partner introduces new but troubling words and games into a relationship, the other has the right to refuse to participate. When Frank asked Mindy to use sexually explicit language, she felt guilty. Instead of repeating the offending words and phrases Frank suggested, Mindy could suggest that they invent a sexually tantalizing language of their own. They could invent pet names for each other's body parts. A conversation that suggests that Frank put "Peter" into Mindy's "Secret Garden" can not only be sexually stimulating, but it is something intensely personal that they could both share.

SPEAKING OF SEX . . .

It is important for Mindy to reassure Frank that she loves him very deeply. After the birth of a child, a woman may suffer a hormonal deficiency which passes in time. Her desire for sex may be temporarily diminished during this period. A man may feel very anxious to resume sexual activity. Mindy needs to explain this to Frank, and ask him to be patient. Meanwhile, she should make a point of showing him how much she loves him.

Mindy and Frank also need to find more time to be together *alone.* When there are young children involved, this is very difficult but not impossible. Sitters are available for evenings out. Friends or relatives can be asked to watch the children for a weekend. Mindy could also suggest something a little more creative. She could plan to meet Frank for lunch . . . in a motel. Her initiative in scheduling this mid-day rendezvous would certainly not make Frank think of her in maternal terms.

Mindy realized that Frank wanted to view her as a sexual person and not as a "mommy." "How is that possible at this time in our lives?" Mindy inquired. "I spend every waking minute when I am not in the office being a 'mom.' How am I supposed to act sexy? I can't even remember what that feels like."

Mindy needs to think of herself as a sexual person once again. Admittedly, she is never alone. It is rare when she can find the time to fix her hair or even glance into a mirror. Mindy needs to *schedule* time for herself, just as she does for her family's appointments. Five minutes in the bathroom each morning, before the children are up, could give her time to fix her hair and put on some lipstick. Mindy could make a point to dress each day as though she is expecting company. After all, she is. Her husband! This could mean wearing something as simple as comfortable jeans and a pretty T-shirt. Today's women are fortunate that sexy clothing can be purchased in half-price stores for very little money. Designers plan their entire collections around T-shirts and jeans.

Mindy could telephone Frank at the office during the day to tell him he can anticipate some special intimate time alone together that evening after the children are asleep. When he hears Mindy's sensual voice whisper her invitation to a sex date that evening, the smile on his face could last for the entire day.

When a couple is making love, ideally there will be many teasing delays and tantalizing kisses and caresses. When little people call out in the night for a drink of water or come tiptoeing into the bedroom, a partner can be left limp—and not with pleasure. There are excellent studies that show locking the *parents'* bedroom door, *not the child's* is an effective way of avoiding interruptions. When the children are older, firmly requesting a knock before entering is a method parents may employ to ensure privacy. Maintaining a sense of humor and planning excursions to area motels are some realistic techniques that will provide privacy and ensure at least some amount of time for couples to spend together. These solutions should work until the children are old enough to understand that, "No, you can't come in Mommy and Daddy's bed unless you are invited," really means "No."

It is helpful for parents to remember that children do grow older. While waiting, it is most important to keep sexual desires alive, so that when personal time is not such a problem, partners will still want to sexually explore and communicate with each other.

CHAPTER 11

Changing Sexual Patterns

Partners in most long-term relationships must at one time or another face the challenge of adjusting to growth and change in their mates and in themselves. No matter how compatible they may be, each partner is bound to possess characteristics that fluctuate with time. A passionate partner who enjoyed a lusty sex life before marriage might evolve into a maternal figure for whom a hot session between the sheets now seems ludicrous. A teasing, inventive, torridly sexual mate might become a rover searching for yet another conquest after the marriage ceremony.

Although changing patterns are sometimes welcomed by partners, they can cause strife in even the most contented of relationships. As is the case with any problem, this strife most often will spill over into the sexual aspect of the relationship. Partners with a satisfying sex life can lose interest in sex or feel disappointment and discontent. They often wish for their partners to "be the way they used to be."

In reality, though, no one stays the same forever. It is normal and healthy for everyone to grow and change. A husband who is disappointed with the changes in his wife's sex drive over the years must realize that in all probability he, too, has changed. A woman who longs for the romantic man her partner was when they first met must realize that their relationship has evolved into a different stage which may be much more satisfying in other ways. In the long haul, partners need to be prepared to make allowances and adjustments for each other.

FROM THE PRESSURE COOKER AND INTO THE BEDROOM
Today's woman often feels she is pressured into endless activity. She feels the need to be all things to all people, and she is often overwhelmed by the stress. Her role is less defined than that of her mother, which can cause great confusion to herself and her mate. Equal rights have brought her even more responsibilities. Where her responsibilities end and her partner's begin are often blurred and confounding.

A common problem for today's assertive woman is that almost all of her energy is absorbed by her career and taking care of her family. That leaves a woman little time and vigor for sex. Often the excitement and mobility of a career and a family prevent a woman from contemplating the state of her sex life, until something specific happens and it can no longer be ignored.

Barrie came for counseling when her husband announced one evening that he was tired of feeling lonely and unloved. He wanted Barrie to pay more attention to their marriage or he was going to do something about it. This vague threat brought Barrie to seek advice. She honestly felt they had a good marriage and was completely surprised by her husband's ultimatum.

THINGS CHANGE, NOTHING STAYS THE SAME
Barrie confided in therapy that she and her husband, Marcus, shared an intoxicating and rewarding sex life at the beginning of their relationship. They could never get enough of each other. Couples envied how they seemed to share some secret knowledge even though they had been together for some time. She laughed at all his attempts at humor. He listened to her every word as though it contained some magical message. Each seemed to possess a playfulness of spirit and an unlimited capacity for devotion. Now, eleven years later, sex is infrequent and uninspiring. A certain comfort level with their intimacy has developed. Neither partner has been showing any noticeable dissatisfaction until Marcus' outburst.

> "Marcus and I met at a medical convention in St. Louis. He is an obstetrician and I am a science writer. I was immediately drawn to his outlandish sense of humor. I had interviewed

countless physicians over the years. Although most of them are experts in their field, they often lack a sense of humor about themselves that I find attractive. At this convention, I was having coffee with the keynote speaker when the man sitting next to us in the hotel dining room asked if I had dropped my notepad. I looked up to find a great-looking man in a brown cashmere jacket holding out a hotel notepad with writing on it. It could have been mine, so I took it from him. On the pad was scrawled, 'Meet me for dinner in the hotel lobby at seven.' It was signed, 'Marcus Welby, M.D.' While I was deciphering the difficult handwriting, the handsome man got up and left. I was so flustered, I could hardly concentrate on coherent conversation with my coffee companion. Throughout the rest of the day, my thoughts continuously drifted to the incident at breakfast and the attractive stranger. Would I meet him at seven? Should I?

"What intrigued me the most about Marcus (whose last name was not Welby) was that he possessed a playful spirit. When I did arrive in the hotel lobby at seven, the joyful look on his face told me I had at last met someone creative and very brave. After all, I might not have shown up. He was obviously not afraid of rejection.

"'Do you invite all your dates for dinner in such an unusual manner?' I inquired. 'What if I hadn't shown up? Isn't approaching a perfect stranger like that rather risky?'

"Marcus told me he had been watching me interview his colleagues for three days. He knew that if he left a request for a date at the message center, I would not have responded. Time was running short. The conference was almost over. So he had asked the hostess in the coffee shop for a table next to mine and conjured the ruse that had succeeded in challenging my curiosity. I was here, wasn't I?

"Although we lived in different cities, we had a lot in common. We discovered we both enjoyed foreign movies and backpacking. We had both been in previous relationships. Marcus had found these affairs stifling. 'I'm just not ready to settle down. My life is too unpredictable. I have lots of things to work out.' was what he always told a lover when she demanded a commitment.

"'That's funny,' I confided, 'I've had the same experience in reverse. I've never met a man who put as much effort into his love relationships as his golf handicap or his career.'

"Months passed. After accumulating staggering amounts of

frequent flyer mileage, we agreed. No one else seemed to interest either of us. While skiing in Aspen that Christmas, Marcus
proposed. I could write my articles anywhere, so I moved. We
married that spring and now have two lovely children. Eric is
nine and Felicia is seven. Marcus' practice has grown. I travel
frequently for a national magazine. Our friends are interesting
and our children bring us both joy. There is just one problem:
our love life is as exciting as boiled chicken."

I'VE GROWN ACCUSTOMED TO YOUR FACE

Barrie continued with her story, relaying that it was very difficult for
her to understand what happened to her marriage.

"We have both grown tremendously as caring, productive people. Marcus is still the person I enjoy being with more than anyone else I have ever met. He is supportive of my career and
wonderful with the children. Why has our sex life become so
stale and monotonous?"

There is nothing new about the corollary between commitment
and boring sex. Passion itself is an emotion aroused by expectation
and inconsistency. When couples become exclusive lovers, this very
same security and stability does not encourage sexual excitement.
Patterns of lovemaking become predictable. A mate knows what
turns a partner on and what the response will be. There is no mystery, no unknown challenge, no surprise.

It is important to remember that in most relationships, sexual
satisfaction is cyclical. It ebbs and flows over the years. There is a
certain familiarity that occurs even when the partners still feel passionate about each other. Various sexual moods are an integral part
of a long-term relationship. Sometimes it is important to be tender.
Sometimes sex is about deep love and connection. There are times
sex is aggressive and times it is sensual. There are times couples engage in just plain old-fashioned lust. If a partner is sensitive to
where a mate is, sex can feel *good* and *different* and *new* all the time.
Of course, consistency is very important. So are love, warmth, humor, respect, and acceptance toward a willing partner. Equally critical is that each partner has the freedom to initiate sex or to say

when the mood is not right at the moment. Freedom of expression insures a mate will not feel rejected. There are certain tricks only one partner need interject into the relationship to keep a marriage from stagnation and restore the mystery and surprise.

LIFESTYLES OF THE SEXUALLY DEPRIVED

When lifestyle is the problem and couples do not *make* the time to relax together, the physical, sensual side of a relationship can disappear. When couples find themselves too busy to schedule this time, their sex drive literally shrivels up and dies. They may begin fearing their own performance. They start to avoid sex or engage in sex expediently and routinely just to get it over with.

Barrie had stopped thinking, caring, or fantasizing about anything to do with sex because she felt she had no time that was not programmed. Marcus, too, was definitely experiencing the result of a complete absence of erotic interest. When they did make love, each turned away from the other and went to sleep immediately after.

Barrie and Marcus had established a solid relationship and viewed themselves as very happily married. As tired as Barrie might be, she did not want to refuse Marcus, so they often made love without enthusiasm. He was concerned that the lack of a vigorous sexual interest on Barrie's part signaled problems in the marriage. Too much worry and concentration was being placed on the absence of time. More energy needed to be used in developing a more exciting sex life for the limited occasions this couple was able to enjoy sex.

Barrie needs to develop a priority list. She loves to read, to backpack, and to ski. So does Marcus. Why then is she putting sex on the bottom of the list? Is she thinking of sex as the last thing to do at night, when both partners are exhausted? If sex is important to Barrie, then why is she too tired for sex but not too tired to worry about the article she is writing that month or the cookies she is baking for Felicia's school event? Most probably, Barrie and Marcus are under stress. Experts agree, when couples are under extreme pressure, sex is the first activity to suffer.

Barrie needs to ask herself what else is bothering her. By her own admission, Marcus is an excellent father. But does he help her with household duties? Is Barrie feeling some resentment toward Marcus of which she is not aware? Perhaps he did not side with her when her mother-in-law suggested that Barrie might be away from the children too much? Is this resentment causing her to hold back from Marcus' sexual advances? Pleading fatigue can be a symptom of personal problems and unresolved difficulties. After Barrie has determined these are not the reasons for this couple's sexual cooling, she needs to face the fact that if she does not do something to change it, their sex life will be perfunctory for years to come. Once these patterns are established, they are difficult to alter.

CHANGE IS GOOD

Barrie and Marcus usually go to bed at 11:30 p.m., after the news. They alarm goes off at 7:00 a.m. In the interest of better sex, they might retire a few hours earlier and set the alarm for an hour earlier. That extra hour in the morning would provide the rested partners time for sex before the children were up and the demands of the day began.

Barrie could ask Marcus if he would mind being awakened during the night for sex, even if it meant resetting the alarm. This can often create new excitement in a static sexual relationship. There is something romantic and almost clandestine about partners waking each other in the middle of the night and enjoying each other's undivided attention.

The most productive thing that Barrie could do to revive their sagging sex life would be to ask Marcus what he would like. Being careful not to conduct an interview, Barrie could involve him in a warm, teasing conversation about what he likes in bed. Even though they have been together for years, she may not realize that he prefers one sexual technique to another. If he asks her if she is writing a book, she could answer "Yes," and it is all about him!

Men are not the only ones who are confused about what a woman wants in bed. Women are, too! This is really not surprising, considering that both want different things at different times. That is what makes making love so interesting and invigorating. Sometimes a woman wants a man to be in total command of the sexual situation. Other times, when the woman wants to be the aggressor, the surprise alone can interject excitement into an otherwise ordinary sexual encounter. The trick here is that it is usually necessary to allow the man to feel he is the leader in the bedroom. Even when the woman is the aggressor, most men need to feel it is with their permission. This is a particularly sensitive and important point for a woman to understand. She may have initiated sex, and he may love it, but he still needs to feel he is "top gun" in order to generate that feeling of potency to which men universally respond.

BEST FRIENDS

"I don't know what has happened to my marriage, but my friends seemed to figure it out." The gorgeously attired woman seeking sexual counsel was actually the internationally known food personality, Joanne Carter, creator and president of Joanne's Gourmet Foods. Constantly interviewed in magazines from *Fortune* to *Bon Appetite*, Joanne was highly regarded as a woman who had crashed through the glass ceiling. Universities bestowed honorary degrees upon her. Wall Street was graced by her company's presence.

> "When my friend, Mary, confronted me last weekend, I was totally shocked. I had no idea she could analyze what was wrong with my marriage when I could not. I was aware something was wrong with Steve's and my relationship, but I thought I had been presenting such a good front that even our closest friends were deceived. After mulling over some of the things that she said, I decided it was time to get some professional help.
> "I was not at all popular in school, nor could I cook. I was never invited to proms or parties when I was young. I was tall and skinny and had brown hair that wouldn't keep a curl. My clothes were hand-me-downs from cousins in another city or something my mother found on sale. I would fantasize about the popular boys in my class and pray that one would ask me out. No one ever did. After graduation, I took a job as a bookkeeper at the local dairy. I often felt lonely. When I was twenty, my mother remarried. I felt uncomfortable living in the same house with them. I knew they wanted and deserved their privacy. I answered an ad in the back of a magazine, and headed

for Chicago with my one suitcase and my head full of dreams.

"The job turned out to be a hoax. I needed work—fast. There was a small restaurant near my apartment with a sign in the window for a cook. I took the job. Although I had no previous experience, I found I loved working in a kitchen. Soon, to make extra money, I was selling my own baked goods to the restaurant customers. Well, one day, one of my customers invited me to dinner. He was very good looking and about ten years older than I. I thought this was just a date, but it turned out to be a business proposition. He offered to set me up in a small baking business for 50 percent of the profit. Someone with that much confidence in me was not to be ignored. The rest, as they say, is history.

"The good looking man who offered to set me up in business has been my husband of eighteen years. Though it was a very unusual way of asking for a date, Steven thought that if we had something to talk about other than the weather, I might become more interested in him. He never suspected he was offering me the realization of a dream. I wanted to be someone who was independent and respected. I had few tools at my disposal. When he gave me the opportunity, I jumped at it. After the lease was signed on my first little kitchen, I called Mary and asked her to come to Chicago and be my right hand. She was unhappy in school and was delighted with my offer. Not only did it mean we would be working together, we would resume the close friendship we had shared for so many years. Eventually, Mary met someone through our company that she married. The business, as you know, has flourished. Everyone seems to have gotten exactly what they dreamed about."

THE PRINCE OR THE BIG BAD WOLF?

"That is why I was so startled by Mary's confrontation. Mary said that Steven acted more like a father to me than a husband. She accused me of behaving like I was still a poor, underprivileged little girl playing dress up and being eternally grateful to my rescuer. She wondered if Steven and I ever had sex, and she had the nerve to ask how, at my age, I could stand being told what to do and how to do it. At first, I thought she was just jealous because her own marriage was such an unhappy one. Then, I realized she touched a nerve.

"Steven has been very good to me. He has become my very best friend. Not only is he an excellent business advisor, he is completely understanding about my long hours and hectic schedule. Except for the baking, he has taught me almost everything I know. We travel from city to city promoting 'Joanne's Gourmet Foods,' and now we have a frozen food line that is distributed throughout the country. Our marketing department has me booked on talk shows constantly to promote our new products. Steven is always there for moral support.

"Steven is extremely proud of all the changes that have taken place in my life over the years. Remember, he knew me when I was a waitress in a small diner selling homemade baked goods on the side. He always shops with me for the expensive clothing I can now afford. He is appreciative of my glamorous look and generous with his compliments. We have the social life I used to dream about, lavish dinner parties and fabulous trips to exotic places. The respect and admiration I yearned for as a child is now mine.

"There is only one problem. Steven and I seldom have sex anymore. When we do, it is in the same old way. I meet so many interesting men in my travels that seem to find me attractive. I flirt with them a little. Steven finds this amusing and is always civil to them. Of course, I would never think of cheating, even if he were not there. But, this lack of sexual intimacy with Steven is frustrating. I have tried to deny these feelings. I suppose I feel guilty for having these thoughts at all. Where would I be without Steven? He has made everything possible for me. I am the perfect wife in every other way and he seems completely satisfied. But, now that I have turned forty, I wonder if I will ever enjoy that sexual intimacy with my husband that other women talk about so glowingly."

REMEMBER WHAT INVOKED LOVE IN THE FIRST PLACE
Joanne had married her best friend. Steven had replaced Mary as the person she most cared about in the world. He was the prince charming she had been waiting for. It was equally easy for Steven to fall in love with Joanne. She was unaware of her sexiness, unlike most young women he had met. Her unassuming fragility brought out the manliness in Steven. He wanted to protect her and to become completely involved in her life. She listened to him, enthralled with his advice and his gifts. No other woman before had responded to him in this way. He was Henry Higgins and she was Eliza Doolittle.

But unlike Eliza, it took Joanne years to realize that something important was missing from their marriage.

Most successful marriages are between partners who consider themselves each other's best friend. Friendship, however, is only one important aspect of a loving relationship. Whereas friendships are based on shared characteristics and goals, sexual desire is aroused because of qualities that are different and intriguing.

Joanne and Steven engaged in frequent sexual activity when they were first married. What had aroused sexual feelings then that now lay dormant and need to be revived? Joanne needs to remember what attracted her to Steven sexually in the very beginning. She needs to visualize how handsome she found him and how strong he felt when she wrapped her arms around him. He still seems generous with his compliments to her and is supportive in her career. What did he say to her intimately when they were in bed together that made her want to make love to him?

Both Joanne and Steven have created a successful enterprise that has become the major focus of their lives. It is energizing for any relationship to have an intense mutual interest. It is destructive to sexual feelings when the outside endeavor overshadows the personal relationship and drains a couple of all the available vitality.

Joanne and Steven are fortunate enough to be on the same conversational wavelength. Unfortunately, Joanne is not sending Steven the message the she longs for him to behave more sexually toward her. She needs to tell him clearly and directly that she is interested in more frequent sex. This couple needs to talk more about feelings, and less about business. Joanne might surprise Steven by initiating sex. Because he might be startled by her unexpected advances at first, she should proceed slowly. By pleasing Steven in the bedroom just as he had pleased her in the past, Joanne could show him how much she cares. Initiating sex could be the electric shock that this couple's sex life so badly needs.

At first, Joanne might find it difficult to reverse roles, but they also might find it refreshingly stimulating. The important issue is that they discuss what they both would like. In their business it is important to be aware of what the market desires. Steven and

Joanne know they have a successful product by the response of the buyers. Now they need to be more responsive to each other's needs. Joint negotiation is what they are great at, so there should be no need for one partner to tell the other what to do. The probabilities for the successful recapturing of an adventurous love life are excellent when partners are concerned for each other's feelings above all else.

YOU'RE NOT THE PERSON I MARRIED

No couple who begins a relationship together in their twenties relates to each other in the same way at forty. All individuals mature, but partners do not necessarily mature at the same pace. Individual, personal experiences can complicate relationships. Even when a relationship is in trouble, the problems might not be experienced in the same way by each of the partners. A sexual pattern that might have worked for years can suddenly seem sour to one of the mates. It is very difficult to express sexual displeasure to a loving partner. Yet, an honest relationship requires mates know exactly where each lover is so that a truly loving response may occur. Couples usually choose mates to create and share a personal world. The sexual aspect is probably the most dynamic force in the relationship. If lovers choose partners who reflect how they see themselves, then when a partner's personal image changes problems can occur.

Deidre, thirty-two, sought counseling shortly after her first wedding anniversary. Her husband, Dean, seven years younger, had been "going out with boys" after they had been working out together at the gym. Deidre, who pretended to be sleeping when Dean came home, was deeply concerned that her marriage was threatened. She could not help but notice the liquor on Dean's breath when he would come to bed. Last week she had identified a perfume that was not hers on his sweatshirt.

> "Dean and I dated for two months before we got married. We met at a gym. He was a real hunk that all the girls watched and drooled over. I was turning thirty-one at the time and did not want to gain any weight, so I was working out judiciously. I watched Dean, too, along with my friends, but I never thought

he would ask me out. After all, I was an older woman. He was a kid of twenty-four."

Deidre explained how she had difficulty learning how to operate the machines in the gym, and Dean had offered to show her how to use them correctly. She was very grateful for his help and offered to buy him a beer after their second session. He accepted and that first beer led to frequent dates that included some dancing and lots of heavy sex.

"Dean was not only a jock in the gym, he was great in the backseat of a car. He began taking me home earlier and earlier, but I could never invite him in, since I still lived with my parents. One night he took me home in his father's new Chevy. That night we had parked in a deserted school yard and had a long, making-out session. The car had electric seats. Dean thought it was so cool to put the front seats all the way back, so we could make out in the front and the backseat. He kept teasing me by moving the seats when I least expected it. The controls were on his side of the car. It was very late, so we decided it was time for Dean to take me home. However, when Dean tried to put the seats back up, they would not budge. He had burned out the motor, or something like that. It was really funny to watch him drive, because he had to sit on the edge of the seat the whole way home.

"Dean was sort of wild and loved to take risks. I had never taken risks. After all, I was thirty-one and still living at home. The sex was fun and quick and very energetic. We knew we couldn't keep up our school yard romance, so we married late that summer.

"Now I find that intercourse goes on much too long for me. Dean prides himself on his ability to last for hours. His thrust sometimes feels relentless to me. Dean loves the feeling of total control. Sometimes he will not ejaculate at all, even at the end of a very long session."

Deidre described how she became extremely sore. She had frequent bladder infections and suffered from skin irritations. She was unable to have orgasms with Dean now that they were in their own home. This was puzzling to her, because she had no problem in the backseat of a car. Since she was unable to have orgasms, Deidre had been looking for ways of avoiding sex with Dean. Dean had begun to stay out late and avoided coming home.

When a relationship is based on sexual activity alone, interruptions in patterns that are not long-standing can be disastrous. Deidre needs help with her marriage in more ways than one. If she does not seek counseling quickly, she might never have the opportunity to establish a meaningful, long-term relationship with Dean. She needs to get his attention immediately.

Instead of avoiding his sexual advances, Deidre needs to reaffirm in loving, caring words that she thinks Dean is terrific. She needs to tell him how much she admires his staying power. She can gently explain to Dean that more is not necessarily better.

Deidre needs to tell Dean that since he is so well-endowed and so firm, she becomes very sore and irritated after awhile. Deidre could suggest they try numerous positions to find one that would give her more control over the movement. She needs to ask Dean to be gentle and understanding with her and follow her signal when she starts to feel uncomfortable. She could suggest and even initiate some intimate alternatives of touching and holding when intercourse becomes too uncomfortable for her. She might ask her gynecologist for a prescription for a lubricant that will be more effective than what she is using. There are many new lubricants on the market. Deidre needs to plan to rest after sex (not necessarily sleep) so that her body recovers.

During therapy, Deidre learned that there was really nothing wrong with her, a fearful thought that kept her awake at night. If the same spot is repeatedly punched on a body with a fist, the body becomes sore. Many women feel this bruising with prolonged intercourse. Because a man might not be aware of this problem, he needs to be told in a sensitive, loving way. Deidre could also gently explain that intercourse may often be the most difficult way for a woman to experience orgasm. She could suggest that they experiment with manual or oral stimulation.

The ability to devise creative, mutually-satisfying solutions to both big and small problems can be a couple's great asset. Experimenting together can help to bring excitement to any relationship, as well as greater understanding. Before this will work, however, partners must have attained mutual trust.

As Deidre and Dean are learning, strong and lasting sexual relationships are based on genuine caring and interest. Just as it takes time to build trust with another person, it takes repeated experience to learn to depend on one another. Great relationships are like sparkling diamonds: they grow stronger and more beautiful with time and endurance.

CHAPTER 12

Love and Sex:
Risky Business

Chances are a woman may be involved with a man who looks like average guy John Goodman, but she'll risk almost anything if he behaves like sex symbol Mel Gibson in the bedroom. Risk is feeling. It takes real courage to face problems directly and experience the pain that is so often involved. But partners who discipline themselves can learn to relish each other rather than fear the risk involved in intimate relationships. Those couples who do risk feel more alive and loving than couples who avoid challenge. It is possible to *learn* to feel and then to express those feelings which result in loving sex. Most experts agree that the depth of a partner's feeling is directly related to the amount of effort extended in a relationship. One key factor seems to be discovering what partners really want from each other. That doesn't mean couples always need to fulfill each other's desires. What it does mean is having the fortitude and determination to make the personal relationship top priority in a couple's life.

Whenever one partner begins a new approach toward another, it is a venture into the unknown. When a lover introduces something new into a relationship or confronts an existing problem, it must be expected that some risk will be involved. But the only alternative to taking risks is to remain stagnant in a relationship. If one partner denies reality by refusing to discuss problems or to work on difficulties, it is sometimes possible for that mate to be temporarily convinced that nothing is really wrong. Almost all partners want to believe their relationship is solid and that it will endure. It is certainly understandable that partners wish to maintain this fantasy. But sooner or later this myth will explode. When a relationship is fragmented, it is often too late and too difficult for it to be restored.

Most partners exercise denial. Some of the time this can be constructive. Concentrating on a relationship's strengths rather than on its weaknesses and focusing on what is right rather than on what is wrong can often help couples to successfully work through difficult periods that all partners experience during the course of a relationship. It is only when a lover's sensitivity becomes numbed and emotional realities are denied that partners will find themselves in difficulty.

To be fully alive means to take risks . . . and risks can feel frightening. Often a mate will fear he or she lacks the strength to try something different. Many are overwhelmed by the dread of imagined consequences. But no partner will ever know how different things might be, or how strong mates can become, until an attempt is made and positive steps are taken to change the problems in an unhappy relationship.

MY WAY

A man may very often feel his mate is only interested in doing what she wants to do and not at all interested in pleasing her partner. Since a woman may spend most of her waking hours planning all the aspects of a couple's life from feeding and clothing to social activities, she is sometimes taken completely by surprise to hear that her mate thinks that she is taking him for granted. This realization may come to a woman's attention from an unusual source, often when she is least expecting it. Such a woman was Lola, who had been in therapy for quite some time before she realized what was really going on in her relationship.

"I watched this television program the other day and I think I learned more from it than I have from my therapy sessions." she said on a recent visit.

> "There was this talk show where four men on a panel discussed what their partners do that turns them off. Every guy on that program said it made him angry when his wife ignored his

feelings about what he wanted. All four agreed that it seemed to them that their mates were only concerned about themselves most of the time. One man complained his wife came to bed in one of his old, torn sweatshirts, no matter how many times he asked her not to. She said wearing this old shirt was comfortable for her, and what she needed at the end of a hard day was to feel cozy and relaxed. Then she was able to sleep better. Another panelist said his wife served meatloaf every Tuesday, even though he complained repeatedly that this was his least favorite dinner. His mate's excuse was that ground meat was inexpensive and helped to stretch the household budget. Besides, the children loved it. Another man reported how his mate only wore makeup when they were going out or if company was coming. The rest of the week she said she didn't have time to bother with it. This man said he felt his partner didn't think that he was important enough for her to look her best."

Sounds simple enough. We all want what we want when we want it. That doesn't mean we always get our way, or give up on a relationship when we don't. If all our wishes from our mates were fulfilled, we would not be enticed for very long.

Lola mused aloud during her session, "After watching that program, I wondered if maybe one reason I have difficulty making my relationship work is because I do put my needs first? You know, I really resent having any man tell me what to do and how to do it."

During the course of her therapy, Lola was beginning to realize the importance of considering a partner's needs. She was also learning that it is not always necessary to put those needs first. There is a subtle difference between being exploited and choosing to behave in a way that gives both partners pleasure most of the time, while still maintaining individual integrity. Learning to distinguish what to do and when to do it does require taking a risk at times. But having faith in one another's ability for love and caring can provide the safety net needed to cushion any long-term relationship.

DOES IT HAVE TO BE THIS WAY?

When Billie Jean sought counseling for an unhappy marriage after four years, she explained she never imagined she would need to seek the advice of a therapist. Billie Jean was a counselor in her church where she consulted with young couples for several months before they took their vows. Trained as a social worker, Billie Jean's services were sought by countless couples who felt her sensitive, caring advice gave them a stronger start in their own marriages.

Billie Jean shared that during courtship she found Herb to be the ideal mate.

"He talked a lot and shared his hopes and dreams with me, no matter how inconsequential. Yet, he seemed equally interested in my aspirations, encouraging me to open a private practice for premarital counseling instead of continuing as a volunteer at my church.

"While we were dating, we spent most of our time in exclaiming how wonderful we thought the other was. We were enthralled with our own feelings of specialness and thought we were perfectly matched. Herb and I were considerate, thoughtful people who shared our lives with many friends and a large, boisterous family. We were thrilled to be marrying each other. Our lovemaking was frequent and passionate, and our communication seemed extraordinary. I had never been with a man who was so open or seemed so sensitive to my needs.

"Things have certainly changed over the four years of our marriage. Herb works very hard, and when he comes home from the office, he is tired and just wants to read the paper and have a good dinner. When I bring up topics to discuss or activities I'd like for us to do together, he seems bored now and much more interested in watching television than in talking to me. We really don't argue. It is just that I feel I'm not very interesting to him anymore. I always have the feeling that I have done something wrong. Either the dinner is not good enough or I have done nothing intriguing enough during the day that he would want to hear about. We seldom make love. I don't feel passionate toward Herb, and he doesn't seem to miss our sex life. We are polite strangers and have behaved this way toward one another for quite some time. I would love to try something new to add some spice to our sex lives, but I worry about Herb's response. I do not want to stay in a dead-end relationship. Maybe I expect too much. Maybe this is what all marriages become once the initial passion is gone. I'm afraid, and I don't know what to do."

Billie Jean and Herb were stuck. Although all the ingredients for a successful marriage were there at the beginning, a relationship is a living thing and needs nourishment to maintain its strength and to flourish. If Billie Jean and Herb were feeling bored with their relationship, perhaps they had allowed themselves to become boring. It is important for each partner to take responsibility for their own sexuality, and not to just be passive receptors. Billie Jean needed to rediscover what gave her pleasure, both in and out of the bedroom, and to show Herb what made her feel sexual. The more she learned about herself, the more she would be able to share with her partner.

Billie Jean might ask Herb what made him feel sexual and responsive. This couple needed to continuously tell *each other* what excited them. In the beginning of this relationship, Billie Jean and Herb gave each other pleasure by revealing and sharing their private thoughts. They indulged in their mutual appreciation of each other's uniqueness. The very newness of sharing their thoughts and their bodies with each other really turned them on. When this fresh and exciting anticipation diminished after marriage, Billie Jean and Herb seemed afraid to share their intimate feelings or any new sexual pleasure with each other. When Billie Jean was able to risk Herb's possible displeasure by openly discussing what was really happening in their relationship, things definitely changed for the better.

Billie Jean had read a little and was interested in learning more about the practice of tantra, an ancient discipline which embodies sex not only as a biological function but as a sacred, divine ritual between lovers. The goal of tantra is to enjoy a slow buildup of sexual energy repeatedly before coming to climax. For many couples, this practice can result in a wonderful feeling of intimacy. She wanted Herb to derive pleasure from a passionate shared experience, but Billie Jean was afraid to introduce this possibility to Herb because she feared he would think it too exotic and Billie Jean weird. Billie Jean was eventually able to risk explaining to Herb that tantra is for intimate partners to practice before retiring in complete privacy with no sense of rushing. Herb was intrigued by the fact that tantra involves concentration and meditation. Both partners learned to relish the slow, seductive building and ebbing of sexual movements with no urgency to orgasm. Herb, as well as Billie Jean, was surprised by the untapped emotions they were able to share. The risk Billie Jean took in introducing something completely new caused these partners to experience a joy and sexual energy that they might never have known. It takes fortitude and trust, but risk is what gives life its spontaneity.

THE SECOND TIME AROUND

With the current divorce rate at approximately fifty percent, there are many divorced men and women who would like to meet someone new with whom they might form an affectionate attachment. Because all men and women enter new relationships with emotional baggage and everyone is afraid of being hurt, it is very arduous for either sex to willingly place him or herself in a vulnerable situation. It takes a certain amount of risk to put one's self "out there." Meeting someone with whom to share a relationship has almost always been difficult for men and women under any circumstances. No one wants to wear a sign proclaiming availability. Other people may pretend to be involved in a relationship so that they feel less valuable. These self-imposed barriers often prevent potential partners from ever getting to know one another.

Sara, forty-one and recently divorced, met Elliot in a computer class. She wondered what he was doing there. Newly unemployed, Sara had applied for a position that required computer literacy, and had enrolled in this course to better her chances.

> "Elliot seemed to comprehend everything the instructor was explaining. I don't understand life, and now I'm supposed to understand these crazy machines? I feel completely overwhelmed. The only thing in that classroom I'd like to learn more about is Elliot. But he probably thinks I'm an idiot. I suppose weeks of this class will go by and we will never even speak other than to say 'hello.' I'm not going to ask him for help. I hate that helpless little female approach. It really gets to me when I see other women use it."

Two weeks later, Sara reported that the instructor had asked the class to share books one evening because students had walked off with some in the previous session. Elliot had moved over to Sara's table and seemed as nervous and uptight as she during the seminar. They concentrated completely on the work at hand and when the class was over, he didn't suggest they go for coffee, though she had hoped he would.

"Maybe he has a wife and three kids waiting at home. I'll never know at this rate. He isn't even that good looking. It's just that my divorce has been final for months now, and no one has asked me out. I feel so lonely. I've rented every current movie at the video store. I have camped out for hours in the frozen food section of the supermarket. All the articles I've read for singles suggest these are great places to meet men. So far, nothing!"

It was easy to understand the loneliness and insecurity Sara was experiencing. Not only was she recently divorced, she was out of work. But she did have some choices. While it was admirable that she was trying to learn how to use a computer to qualify for a new job, there were other employment opportunities out there for which she already possessed some expertise. Perhaps she might apply for one of these while continuing to take her computer class during the evenings. Then, when she became proficient enough and developed some confidence, she might apply for an opportunity in which she would have more chance of succeeding.

Sara's second choice was to search for male companionship, not out of her deep need, but from her sincere interest. She really knew nothing about Elliot, other than the fact he was a man and he was in the same room with her three nights a week. If she approached him because she was interested in who he was and what his interests and thoughts were, rather than for what he could do for her, Sara would have a better opportunity for developing a relationship.

Sara related in therapy that at the end of her last class she invited the members and the instructor to join her for coffee and cake, which she brought to the class in a picnic basket. She briefly explained to her fellow students that since they had shared so many working hours together, she thought it would be nice if they took a few moments to learn something about one another before rushing off to their own lives. Everyone was very pleased at her thoughtfulness. They eagerly shared bits and pieces of their lives with each other. Elliot did have a wife and children, and had recently lost his job. But the retired couple sitting next to her had a newly divorced son, Sam, who was back in town for the first time in years. They invited Sara for Sunday dinner to meet him. It was risky for Sara to accept an invitation from virtual strangers. After all, they had nothing in common besides the computer class, and she had no idea what their son would be like. But she decided to take the risk anyway. Sam turned out to be quite charming. Sara's weekends were now spent with him exploring the city and rediscovering interesting spots they had both forgotten. She took the risk and enriched all their lives.

STRICTLY PERSONAL
There are numerous kinds of relationship risks that can be taken during a lifetime. Sometimes they work out well and other times not so well. It is important to remember that when we face new and unfamiliar situations directly, some pain and legitimate suffering may be involved. These experiences are all part of the process of living. We need to remind ourselves that we are constantly striving to solve life's problems, and we might not always succeed in working them through. Most of the time, with proper caution in mind, risk-taking can make life more exciting and rewarding.

Grace, an attractive woman in her thirties, shared her story of taking a risk that paid off.

"I have been subscribing to a society magazine for years. It's fun to read because it tells me about all the parties in the city to which I'll never be invited and has articles about vacations I'll never be able to afford. I know it sounds like I am living vicariously, but who cares? My own life is so boring. Reading about other people's is at least more interesting and fun.

"When I divorced my husband twelve years ago, I was twenty-six. I had a good job and we had no children. People told me I was very attractive. I felt my marriage was going nowhere. Hal drank a great deal and his dental practice had begun to dwindle. He and I began to lead separate lives. His friends were more intellectual than I was, and I was bored by the theater they chose and the books they discussed. I wanted some excitement, some night life. I began meeting friends after work and exercising several nights a week at an athletic club. Later we would go for a drink and dancing. I never was much of a drinker, but I loved the music in the bars. In those years there was usually a pianist who would play requests. I met lots of interesting people and felt for the first time that I was really part of the world. One of the men I met told me of an excellent job opening in public relations in the city government. He thought I would be perfect for the position. I applied, got the job, and now I run the department. There are constant visitors from out of state as well as from other countries for whom we must get publicity. Our staff has increased greatly over the years. I am never at a loss for activity, but being busy doesn't keep me from feeling lonely. I have not met that one particular person who would make me want to settle down permanently. I am beginning to worry that I never will. That is why I took a personal ad out in this magazine."

Seventy-five responses later, Grace seemed like a different person.

"No, I haven't answered all the replies yet. I'm taking my time. It is almost like having a box of delicious chocolates and choosing just one or two each day to make it last. I requested a photo in my ad, and most of the replies do contain pictures of men. Usually snap shots, but I have received one gorgeous professional photograph. I am saving him for last. The best part of this is that I feel completely safe. The letters come to a post office box, so no one has my address or phone number. I call them. I have met eight men for lunch thus far. I meet them near my office in a crowded public place. At this point no one has interested me enough to accept a real date. But the anticipation does make the day go faster, and with seventy-five responses to acknowledge, my days are filled.

"The funniest part of this story is that a man in my office has asked me out. We have known each other for years. Just last week he told me he never noticed before how much fun I seemed to be. He said I am always smiling and he would like to get to know someone who always seems that happy. We have a date this Saturday."

Some people might think what Grace did was a foolish risk. But Grace knows she has made an important initial step toward broadening her horizons. She has also learned that having an exciting job does not always mean having an exciting life. Many people spend so much of their lives working that they have little time or energy left to develop rewarding personal relationships. If the truth be known, many men and women do not lead balanced lives.

LIFE CAN FEEL LIKE A SEESAW

It is often easy to blame a lack of balance in our lives on the pressures of jobs, families, and society at large. Most people are responders. Men and women react rather than act. Many people do what must be done at that moment, when there are no longer any choices. How many partners are afraid to risk doing what they want to do when they feel the time is right? Many only act when they feel pressured. Some partners expend so much effort in avoiding caring for themselves and their mates that nothing is actually accomplished until uncomfortable circumstances reach epoch proportions. If there is just one thing learned from reading this book, let it be that everyone has choices. It is important to differentiate between out true obligations and responsibilities and the demands we put upon ourselves. We all have lives that are determined by outside forces, but we also have personal needs that are separate from the outside world and belong only to us. This part of our deepest personal existence we must define for ourselves. It just takes insight and planning. Yes, it is risky, but so is the business of living.

WHOSE IDEA IS THIS ANYWAY?

"My husband is driving me crazy!" stated Darla during therapy.

> "He has time and money for everything except me. Have I taken the children for braces, called his mother, invited his boss for dinner, called the plumber, and paid the monthly bills? 'Don't forget to put stamps on the bills,' he admonishes, 'so I can mail them from the office.' Joe has time for everything and is so organized, or rather has me organized. There is never any time for being alone together just talking about the two of us, what we need to do. I feel starved for some loving. I don't just mean sex,

although that would be nice. I mean caressing and kissing and just holding hands. We don't even send each other greeting cards anymore. Joe figured out how much we would save a year if we didn't send cards or give gifts to each other. He has decided these are all commercial holidays anyway, designed to profit the greeting card and candy companies. I don't know. I would love to have the economy improve because I received red roses on Valentine's Day! I know the cost is exorbitant, but it would make me feel better than all the money we've saved."

When I questioned Darla about why she didn't send cards and give small gifts to Joe anyway, she replied she was afraid of risking his anger. "He yells at me when I buy him presents. He thinks it is silly and a waste of money. Even though it is my money from my own job, he tells me he doesn't need gifts. But doesn't everyone need to know he is cared about in some tangible way?"

Two things were going on in this relationship. This couple was exercising habits that emphasized efficiency and practicality at the expense of caring. They were so structured they had lost all sense of spontaneity. Certainly they filled all their waking moments with accomplishments, but they seemed to have done so at the expense of their personal life.

The other phenomenon occurring in this marriage was that one partner felt too intimidated to try to fulfill the perceived needs of the other for fear of risking his anger. Although this couple had developed some bad habits in relating, it would be useless to blame those habits on the pressures of the world around them or materialism or on the demands of their time. The only thing one partner can change is his or her own behavior.

Darla needs to realize that as long as she wishes to buy presents for Joe that he doesn't want and feels are a waste of money (no matter whose money it is), she will probably always incur his wrath. If Darla wants to express her caring through gifts, perhaps she could give Joe something that does not cost money but does show real caring. She could prepare a favorite dinner or knit a great ski sweater, if she sincerely feels she needs to give him something tangible to show her affection. He is certain to appreciate her thoughtful gestures. As for wishing that Joe might buy her expensive flowers on

Valentine's Day, perhaps he will be more likely to respond to the idea when she explains how important this is to her, how it would make her feel.

Realistically most of us realize that we are probably never going to win the lottery, but many of us do continue to hope and to dream about the possibility. We can only change our own habits and our own responses to situations and that is not easy. It takes perseverance and dedication to find new ways to express affection. Is the reward of a more appreciative and contented partner worth the risk? Most of us would say yes.

REALITY CHECK

Sometimes it is important to come to the realization that a relationship cannot work, no matter how hard the partners have tried. The negative feelings in the relationship seem impossible to overcome. Whatever the reason . . . loss of trust, inability to stop blame, continuously feeling like a victim, believing a partner's treatment is unfair, or overwhelming feelings of hopelessness . . . leaving a relationship is a momentous risk. It means reentering the world as an adult alone. Friends will change. Some will disapprove and distance themselves from the mate leaving a relationship. Old reliable patterns will be disrupted and security will disappear. Nevertheless, it is sometimes necessary to take this step. Ellie, a somber-looking woman, confided that this was certainly the most painful decision of her life.

> "Lyle and I have grown very much apart. It is sadly amusing to me that most people think we are the ideal couple. Although I have forgiven his brief affairs over the years and have accepted the fact we will probably always argue about money, I feel angry and unfairly treated most of the time. Our children are grown and married, enjoying rewarding careers and families of their own. I am a student advisor in the high school and love my work. Lyle is a specialty store owner and has been very successful. I suppose we could be described as affluent. We travel frequently and live in a lovely condominium. We both are in excellent health and enjoy our friends and family very much.
>
> "I know there must be something wrong with me, but I feel

empty much of the time. It is not for lack of interests. I love to read and to explore and enjoy being alone as well as with friends. I know that many people experience loneliness because they are not on friendly terms with themselves, but this is not the case in my situation. I feel I am still a vital woman, though certainly not young, and something important is missing from my life. I sense there must be something more out there for me, and I would like the opportunity to see what life feels like without the burden of all this depression and frustration."

What was missing from Ellie's life was not something she could buy or do. It was the sensation of excitement and romance. Ellie wanted to feel she was special. So many partners assume that after a certain age these feelings are no longer necessary or even possible to satisfy. Where did couples get the idea that love and excitement were only for the young? Who ever decreed that spontaneity and sexual fulfillment are needs that diminish as the pages of a calendar are turned?

If one partner decides to end a relationship and to begin a new life after many years of marriage, it is imperative for mates to discuss their feelings with each other clearly and carefully. Sometimes a mate will finally understand the depth of a partner's feelings and realize that, without necessary adjustments, the marriage will end. It is difficult but necessary to share heartbreak with family and friends. The need for their caring as well as for the advice of a professional will become of paramount importance. Ending a relationship, no matter if it is one of thirty years or thirty months, is always a devastating individual decision that needs to be considered very carefully.

A LIFE-LONG ADVENTURE

If you watch an aging couple that people like to be around, it is usually because they have not lost their sense of adventure, their ability to have fun. Nothing is *assumed* by these special individuals. Nothing is completely known. There is always something new for them to learn about each other and the people around them, something more to be appreciated and understood. This same quality of adventure and thirst for deeper understanding is the essence of love, no matter what the age. A partner we thought we knew and understood everything about at twenty is not the same person at sixty. Hopefully that mate has learned a great deal and has been enriched both by experiences and relationships. Often partners assume that once a mate is understood that basic understanding remains for a lifetime. This is usually not the case. People change. Personalities are not established in cement; they are developed over a lifetime. An emotionally satisfying life can be filled with extraordinary, unfamiliar events. Of course, it is risky to attempt something new. But it is that certain amount of risk that keeps us young and desirable, regardless of chronological age.

It is certainly true that we live in a culture where sexuality is suppressed, as well as greatly exaggerated. The prototypes we see around us on television, in the movies, or in the novels we read are almost always based on exceedingly attractive young couples exploring love for the first time. They seem to be ideals and are often the role models many of us choose to emulate. When couples' lives don't turn out to be quite so ideal, it is not unusual for partners to admonish themselves as well as each other. We all aspire to unrealistic perfection. Very few mates seem to recognize that more often than not these couples have absolutely no idea how sexuality really works in a long-term relationship. These models, like most of society, have little concept of how to keep sexual excitement alive. Very few mates expect that during the course of a lifetime commitment, there will be times when there is illness, financial difficulty, problems with raising children, and a multitude of other dilemmas that occur as partners mature and become more aware of life's possibilities.

More often than not, it is extremely difficult to learn how to handle the good times as well as the unhappy times during any long-term relationship. While one partner copes with a particular problem in one way, the other may find a totally different solution. Often one partner may feel hurt and left out if it is not made clear that both care equally but have chosen alternative ways of dealing with these situations. Unless partners are in continual conversation with one another, loving feelings can get lost in a quagmire of misunderstanding. It is not possible for couples to spend a great deal of time together and not make mistakes. It is virtually impossible never to hurt each other's feelings or to misunderstand what one mate may mean by a particular response. All partners need to learn to forgive themselves and each other so that this anger does not fester and grow out of proportion, smothering all feelings of love and desire.

Commitment to a partner is like a contract. But this mutual agreement needs to be renegotiated continuously as the years go by. No one partner can possibly foresee all the unimaginable events that will shape a couple's lifetime. Circumstances change, people change. Those changes are risky. So is love.

CHAPTER 13

The Lover's Bill of Rights

Even the most loving partners with the most sound relationships sometimes experience difficulties in relating to each other sexually. During these painfully arduous times, it is important to remember that when a couple's sex life gets temporarily out of kilter, it does not have to mean the relationship is over. It is possible, even during times of deep emotional stress for mates, to gain an even greater understanding of some of the various ways sexual problems may be resolved. Remember that there are as many variations of couples as there are types of problems. There is no one solution for them all. Couples who are able to communicate with each other will most certainly have a better chance of being able to gain control over feelings of anger, fear, and rejection. When partners learn to focus on the positive aspects of the relationship, love and sex, the winning combination, will have a much better chance of reasserting themselves.

A "Lover's Bill of Rights" can be helpful to almost all couples for those times when one partner or the other changes the contract during a love relationship. In times of difficulty, partners could refer to mutually developed and agreed upon written guidelines that fit the couple's special, individual needs. Often, this will help reinforce connections of love.

Initially, during relationships, a woman assures the man who loves her that she will never change . . . and then she does. Or she may marry a man in hopes he will change . . . and he doesn't. When couples unite, spoken and unspoken sexual and emotional contracts are entered into. Each person brings to the relationship expectations, hopes, fears, and past experiences. These are the "commandments" each partner assumes will not be broken. The anger, hurt, and disappointment he or she may experience along the way usually stems from perceived infringement on one of the commandments, such as:

- Thou shall not change over the course of the relationship.
- Thy career shall not be more important than thy lover.
- Thy mate shall always come first.

To continually renew the love connection and to ignite the sexual spark, couples need to constantly renegotiate their Lover's Bill of Rights.

Remember, no relationship is perfect all of the time. But, by learning some new skills, it is possible for most lovers to reinforce and improve that most special of all connections called love. The majority of people have little difficulty accepting these imperfections in their friends. But when it comes to physical and romantic love, many expect partners to be ideal. Mates often have great difficulty allowing for each other's humanity. Learning how to let go of unrealistic expectations of a mate is difficult, but not impossible.

It is generally acknowledged that "love is blind." When love is new, couples notoriously overlook each other's faults and fantasize about a mate's perfection. This is not surprising. Both sexes are taught from childhood to expect to find perfect love in a mate who will fulfill every desire. Couples fall in love while listening to lyrics of songs that exclaim the impossibility of living without that one special person who creates these rare and unique feelings within. Lovers court in romantic settings and reveal intimate secrets to each other that are not shared with anyone else. It is universally expected that these fabulous feelings of love will remain forever.

Sensual love has been described by experts as the fulfillment of physical gratification. There is a difference between sensual love and love characterized by tenderness. Both kinds of love constitute romantic sexual love. Almost all lovers overidealize a partner in the beginning of a relationship. But, even the deepest love will not be immune to feelings of ambivalence and hostility from time to time.

Couples bring to marriage countless romantic and sexual desires and expectations. All lovers want and expect fireworks. But dry spells often arrive in times of stress and disappointment. Even though a couple may be adept at creating sparks, if negative feelings of anger are expressed often enough, they destroy feelings of sexual bliss. Through sexual love, the ordinary boundaries between man and woman are fused. In order to perpetuate loving unification between mates, partners need to acquire as much insight as possible into each other's needs and feelings.

Love is a subjective experience. True insight into a partner's behavior can only be achieved with constant communication about what mates desire in order to make them feel truly loved. Despite all the information on sex that is available, partners are often unsure of what a mate wants. It is assumed that every woman wants a lover who is tender and caring and who cherishes her above all else. Women generally do adore a man who causes her to feel she is the most fantastic person in the world. Men adore women for the same reasons. When a mate makes a partner's pleasure the highest priority, the partner usually responds with vigorous loving appreciation. But, problems can occur when a partner does not know what triggers a mate's sexual responses. Therefore, it is especially important for a couple to be aware of what turns a partner on and to communicate those sexual feelings to each other in a gentle and caring way.

For such communication to transpire, mates need to be able to express desires in words that are *caring* and *explicit*. It is impossible for partners to read what is on each other's minds, although very often mates try to guess. It is a common fallacy that partners want the same thing at the same time. This is usually not the case.

Most men are aware that women love romance. What romance means to a woman is another story. To one woman romance is a candlelight dinner for two, flowers, and dancing. To another, it may be making love in a sleeping bag under the stars. The one thing on which all women agree is that trust and commitment are necessary for a joyous loving relationship. Once trust is gone, love and sex are never the same for a woman. The ultimate aphrodisiac for a passionate sexual relationship is trust. Without trust, no offer of glamorous gifts or exciting adventures can ever serve to recapture a wondrous sexual commitment.

Although it is certainly true that almost all couples desire an exhilaratingly intimate, loving relationship, few come close to attaining this ideal. Why are love and sex so universally desired and so difficult to attain? Perhaps it is because many partners view love as something to be attained, not something *to do*. If partners can remember that love is a *verb*, almost all mates will be better able to succeed in a satisfying loving relationship. Successful relationships occur when everything a partner *does* and *says* reflects that love. To think of love as a verb means acting out those positive, caring feelings.

In counseling, a frequently asked question is, "What does my partner want?" Clients seem mystified about how lovers want to be treated sexually. There is no magic formula. Excellent advice is for partners to treat each other as he or she *wants* as long as it *feels comfortable to both*. This may seem like clear and simple advice. It is. And it works!

Of course, there are difficulties in consistently practicing this "Golden Rule of Sex." Disillusionment and anger do occur during any long-term relationship. Sometimes partners will pretend not to be hurt or upset. But these very normal feelings will eventually be reflected in the actions between the mates. It is better to deal with these feelings as a couple goes along. An important aspect of successful loving is that partners can *learn* to forgive one another for mistakes, real or imagined. This forgiveness can act as the bridge to loving understanding between couples.

If a partner can love a mate enough not to judge but to *accept who a partner really is* and go on from there, a fulfilling sex life can most certainly be assured. Forgiveness is more important to a relationship than candlelight dinners and sexy nightgowns. While these do have their place as accents to enhance the ambiance during loving interludes, nothing is more sexually potent than the element of forgiveness. To forgive means having a selective memory. Forgiveness is a conscious decision to focus on love and release negative feelings. A partner needs to decide whether it is more important to be *right* or to be *happy*. Anger and frustration are undeniable emotions. Loving partners need to acknowledge these feelings, discuss them, and then, move past them.

Almost all mates wish a lover would spend leisurely, uninterrupted time enjoying sex. Who does not relish a partner who is seductively teasing and sensual in touch and manner? As much as each lover may desire these qualities in a partner, the truth is that it is often difficult to find the time for this mutual enjoyment.

Most mates applaud that the sexual revolution has arrived, at last. Women are beginning to achieve equal rights in the workplace, which often means both partners work outside the home. The down side to this, though, is that both partners are likely to be exhausted most of the time. Interviews with countless couples show that months may go by without any sexual activity between the mates, even for the most compatible of couples.

For most of these two-career families, the dual responsibilities of work and family create so much stress and tension that sex comes very low on the list of priorities. Clients complain they have body parts that have not been used in so long, they feel certain they have atrophied. Women report that when they are aggressively working at their careers during the day in what is still primarily a man's world, they can't even begin to think about sex in the evening when their partners return home. Overwhelming schedules also interfere with a couple's sex life.

After working long hours, sometimes it is "Let's just pick up Chinese," instead of a leisurely dinner where intimate conversation might be exchanged. When work is ended and partners are finally together, it is difficult to leave the pressures and responsibilities behind. How does one stop thinking about the case that needs to be presented in court the next morning or the advertising campaign that must be developed for a new client? Lifestyles are so exhausting, there is almost no energy remaining for making love.

When a person allows his or her physical and sensual side to dissipate, the sex drive likewise disintegrates. If a sexual relationship begins to fail, mates may begin to doubt their sexual performance. Both partners may begin avoiding sex entirely. Often, when the atmosphere between couples becomes negatively charged, counseling is sought.

Victor sought sexual counseling for a marriage crippled by fatigue and lack of interest. He entered therapy after he and his wife, Marlene, found each partner's desire for sex to be waning. Sexual pleasure and being with a loving partner who would not change were high on Victor's Lover's Bill of Rights. He did not know how to renew their contract.

SEXUAL RIGOR MORTIS

"Marlene and I have been married for four years. We met as opposing attorneys on a huge case involving tax law. Marlene's legal abilities were a definite turn-on for me. I am ashamed to confess, before I knew Marlene, I had always been suspect of a woman's capabilities in the courtroom. To me, these women came on so strong, I was completely turned off. Occasionally a woman attorney was so soft-spoken, I felt as though she was using her gender to gain sympathy. I seldom dated women in my law classes. Even after achieving a prestigious position in my firm, my dating tastes centered on very feminine types like fashion consultants and elementary school teachers. I am not proud of my previously chauvinistic attitude. During my single years I felt I had seen enough aggressive females in my practice to know I didn't want a woman who might critique my behavior in the bedroom. Then I met Marlene.

"Marlene was exactly the opposite of any woman I had previously dated. She is very tall, almost as tall as I. She has naturally red hair and freckles all over her body which I find entrancing. She was certainly aggressive during the hearing, but this time I wasn't turned off. I was intrigued. When we left the courtroom and headed for the parking lot together on that last day of our case, Marlene appeared businesslike and eager to return to her office. There was nothing flirtatious about her at all. I found her behavior challenging. After that case ended, I called Marlene and asked her for a date. I had selected a wonderful little French restaurant and planned an intimate dinner so we could get to know each other. Marlene responded to my invitation by saying she had two tickets to a hockey game in town that evening and if I wanted to go with her, she would be delighted. No French dinner. No 'getting to know you' over a bottle of wine and a chocolate soufflé.

"Not one woman in my experience had ever taken the lead in a dating situation. I was fascinated. We went to the hockey game. Weeks later we were enjoying camping together as well as old movies and occasional romantic dinners. I had never felt so strongly about a woman before. I fell madly in love.

"One frosty Saturday evening, while sipping hot toddies in front of a campfire, I asked Marlene to marry me. She refused. She spoke very gently, but Marlene told me in no uncertain terms that she had plans for her career which might include a move to another city in the near future. Marlene explained that she felt she wasn't ready for a family yet. To Marlene, having a family was the only reason for her to contemplate marriage. Although she made it clear that there was no one else in her life, she said she preferred our relationship to remain as it was for the time being. What a jolt to my ego! My first response was to end the relationship. But I cared too much, and so we continued to see each other.

"Our sex life could only be described as fantastic. Marlene had boundless energy and was not shy about initiating sex. Not every time, but just often enough to make our sexual relationship exhilarating and unpredictable. Marlene was completely open and free sexually and I found that very refreshing. I had never been involved with anyone quite like her.

"Marlene's only reason for marriage was that she wanted to start a family. Her biological clock was ticking and I was there when the alarm went off. She became pregnant immediately. Everything changed after our daughter was born. Marlene changed from an erotic mistress to an ethereal Madonna. Her every thought seems centered around our daughter. Kelsy is one and a half, and Marlene is planning on returning to work in one month. Her entire conversation revolves around choosing the proper day care and how exhausted she is. I certainly care about our child's safety. I love her. She is a precious little girl. But, she is all-consuming to Marlene. My wife seems to have no time for me anymore.

"I am seeking counseling not just because I am the usual frustrated husband. I need help because our intimate relationship has seriously diminished. I cannot totally blame Marlene for the decline in our sex life. I do miss her coquettish teasing, but I view her differently now, too. She no longer holds any erotic interest for me, even though she is not pregnant. I see her as a wonderful mother. But I am unable to think of her as my sensual, sexual partner. I know there must be something wrong with me. I don't mean to be insensitive. I just don't know how to revive my sexual feelings toward my wife. Is there any help for me, for us?"

It is not unusual for a once lusty sexual partner to view a mate differently once a child is born. Couples project inner feelings to each other. When this couple first became intimate, Marlene was feeling powerful and creative toward Victor and she expressed these feelings sexually. She was innovative, aggressive, and delightful in her sexual behavior. Now that Marlene is a mother, her foremost reason for marrying, it is her maternal behavior that is dominant and this is what she conveys to her husband. Victor, not unlike most men, has difficulty in making love to a woman he now views in the image of a mother.

Mothers are not supposed to be sexual beings, or so we're conditioned to believe. Since Marlene is the primary caretaker for Kelsy and is planning to return to work while her child is still quite young, she and Victor have not had the time and space to regain a thriving sexual relationship. When sex has been good between partners, it can be taken for granted. Mates expect bells to ring and lights to go off every time. The truth is, reality sets in in any relationship. Great relationships are not guaranteed. They are the result of flexibility, patience, and the ability to communicate. Victor and Marlene need help to get back on the sexual track by engaging in conversation about what each needs and wants.

This couple's sexual expectation needs to be lowered for a while. In order for Victor, who truly loves Marlene, to regain his sexual feeling for her, he needs to take things very slowly. When he approaches Marlene in an intimate time together, Victor must not be expecting orgasm to be the goal. He might take Marlene in his arms and leisurely stroke her body, expecting nothing but his own enjoyment in touching her. Women usually respond to sensual, intimate touch and wish that men were not so obsessed with female orgasm. Intimacy, closeness, and sharing during lovemaking can be mutually satisfying. Of course, eventually both would like orgasms. But, in reestablishing a sexual relationship, sexual play can be satisfying in itself.

Victor needs to help Marlene recapture her sexual feelings. He could reminisce about his favorite sexual encounters with Marlene, and how much he enjoyed her being the aggressor. It is important not to press for climax, just to share the memories. This could rejuvenate Marlene's sexual feelings toward Victor.

Marlene needs to be reassured she is a sexual person and not an object. Victor and Marlene together can rediscover the rest of her body. Victor could try different strokes. Alternating deep massaging motions with light titillating touches, perhaps with a feather helps to stimulate sexual feelings. Kissing and cuddling for generous periods of time help regenerate sexual feelings in a couple before going for the big "O."

It is important to take responsibility for his or her own sexual satisfaction. A woman does not want to feel a man is doing something just to please her without experiencing his own enjoyment. Loving partners want to feel pleasure as well as give pleasure. When this couple is able to relax and enjoy sexual touching, a positive sexual attitude and pleasure are certain to return. Every caring gesture toward a woman helps her feel feminine, special, and loved. Amazingly, when a mate babies a partner, a lover becomes very grown-up, much to the delight of both. It is often said a woman cannot have sex until she feels loved. When Victor is able to tell Marlene how much he has missed her and she is feeling secure and valued as a woman, not only as a mother, her sexual feelings for him will most likely be revived.

SEXUAL LIES

The right to lie to a mate is definitely not included in the Lover's Bill of Rights. Sexual secrets undermine the basis for true communication between partners. Why would a mate lie to a partner? There are numerous reasons. Lying can be a way of guarding against hurt or a habit developed at a young age in order to avoid being mocked or humiliated for exposing private thoughts and dreams. A partner may experience guilt or shame, or feel if this secret were known, a mate would think less of him or her. The reasons for lying are end-less, but they are clearly not acceptable in a loving relationship.

Lavonda had moved seven times before her eighteenth birth-day. Her father was enlisted in the army and served during two wars. He never rose in the ranks because of his constant drinking and fighting. Eventually, he received a dishonorable discharge. La-vonda attended army schools sporadically. Her learning skills were never expanded and after classes she had to rush back to the trailer park where she lived to care for her four younger sisters so her mother could work on the post as a cleaning woman. Lavonda al-ways felt embarrassed at school when she saw the children who lived in the same homes her mother cleaned. The army school was the only school and everyone from the post knew everyone else. Usually no one spoke to her, except to make fun of her drunken fa-ther and her hand-me-down clothes.

When Lavonda's father left the service, he left the family as well. Lavonda took a job in a stockroom in town to help support her mother and younger sisters. Although she earned little, she was able to buy some new clothes and have her hair cut regularly at a beauty shop. After a few months, she stopped sending any money home and no longer visited her family. All communication between them ceased.

Her job in the stockroom was pleasant. It was the first time La-vonda had friends. The young women gossiped while they worked. No one cared as long as they got the work done. For Lavonda, the gossip was heaven. She created a whole new background for herself. These new friends knew nothing about her or her family. Lavonda described at length how her father was killed in Desert Storm and her mother remained home with her four small daughters, trying to recapture her life without a husband.

Lavonda herself did not mind her long hours at work. She loved the small apartment over the dress store where she lived. Even-tually she began to date Kenneth, a young man from the gas station who believed everything she said. They married the day after Thanksgiving, four months after they met. Lavonda told Kenneth he had been her only lover. She never planned to tell him that when she lived on the army post, the only way she had experienced affection was to sleep with anyone who asked her.

No one from Lavonda's family attended the wedding. There were certainly no former friends to be concerned about. Lavonda began what she hoped would be a new, faithful life where she could feel safe and in control. She no longer needed to feel any guilt or shame for her previous behavior. Kenneth and her co-workers knew nothing about her former life.

Years passed before Lavonda sought therapy. The woman who came for counseling was large and placid looking. Her dark hair framed her intense eyes and firmly set mouth. Lavonda seemed shy and very lonely as she entered the office.

Lavonda shared a letter she had just received from one of her sisters who, by now, was in her twenties. The letter informed Lavonda that their mother had died, the girls had all grown, and no one knew where the father was. Her sister, Ceil, was asking Lavonda to send her two thousand dollars to pay for a car she had wrecked, or Ceil would tell Kenneth about Lavonda's past. Pure blackmail. But Lavonda, who had spent the last six years being the perfect wife, was terrified her lies and secrets would be revealed. Lavonda did not have two thousand dollars of her own. If she had, she would have happily sent it to her sister.

"I have suffered panic attacks for years. I have done everything I could to please my husband and keep an emotional distance from everyone so I would not make a slip and allow anyone to know what I am really like. I maintain my privacy and help out in our church. I volunteer in the hospital and spend hours teaching our two children to be polite, respectful, and to complete their homework on time. We are a quiet, respected family. It is true, Kenneth complains now and then that I am not as passionate as he would like me to be. I withhold any inventive, erotic behavior from him. He might wonder where I gained all my sexual expertise. But I am thoughtful and giving. I don't know what I will do if my sister, who obviously knows where I am, destroys the life I've worked so hard to maintain."

Lavonda thought she had separated herself completely from her family. She felt she could afford to take no chances that anyone would upset her life or cause any turmoil.

Lavonda needs guidance to define exactly what her secrets are. With the help of a therapist, she needs to sort out the sexual climate of her early life both within and outside of her family. After taking a long, personal history, the impact of her lies needs to be discussed with a caring professional. Lavonda needs help to determine if her actions are now those of a victim trying to protect the little love and security she possesses, or if she is withholding from her partner to protect her own self-esteem and rationalize all the sensitive issues in her life. Lavonda might be making endless excuses for Kenneth's lack of sexual enthusiasm, or for her own. If Lavonda continues to divert her true feelings and not face her past experiences, they become even more threatening to her in the future. Perhaps her other sisters might not attempt to blackmail her, but Lavonda is living in constant fear that her past indiscretions might be discovered.

Living with a lie often results in painful feelings of bitterness and anger. Lavonda constantly felt she would be rejected if the truth were known. These negative feelings continuously eroded her self-esteem.

With professional help, Lavonda was able to be completely honest with Kenneth. She learned it was possible to express her feelings and develop a more intimate atmosphere with her mate. Kenneth felt the responsibility of alleviating Lavonda's pain. Together, they met with the sister. No further blackmail or threats occurred. All the family members were enriched by reuniting with each other and validating their shared past. Sexual lies cause destructive patterns in relationships that continue for years. The relief of resolution takes courage and commitment that can result in much stronger intimate relationships. Being honest with a mate should rank at the very top of the Lover's Bill of Rights.

ME TARZAN, YOU JANE

When Janice called for an appointment, she warned that trying therapy was her last resort. She needed help with a new development in her marriage. Janice, a successful urban developer in her late twenties, arrived feeling angry. She was dressed in a smart business suit, carrying the requisite designer briefcase.

"Can you imagine me playing docile slave girl to my husband in bed? That sort of behavior goes against everything I stand for. Women have fought long and hard for equality. Who does he think he is? What does he think I am?

"Gregg bought me a harem outfit for my birthday, of all things. And, to top it off, he was hurt and disappointed when I refused to put it on. Imagine? I would never wear a costume like that, even for Halloween!"

Her husband, Gregg, over six feet tall and polished-looking, arrived a few minutes after Janice's initial outburst.

"I did buy her that gorgeous outfit for her birthday. I thought Janice would find it exciting. She spends the entire week in charge of difficult meetings. I thought she would enjoy having someone tell her what to do for a change. Our sex life, when we have any at all, is very mundane. Actually it is boring. I thought it would be fun to dress up and play a little. All I wanted to do was bring a little zest into our sex life."

The dialogue that continued was indicative of their different points of view.

"You just don't understand me at all," Janice admonished. "I like to solve other people's problems. I enjoy being in charge. Clients rely on my advice. I am a competent person, not a submissive slave."

"You could be the master and I could be the slave," countered Gregg.

Janice did not laugh.

"What Gregg considers a sexual turn-on, I find silly and childish," explained Janice. "I have a very difficult profession in which I have worked very hard. The hours are long and my coworkers are often unpleasant. Mine is a very competitive field. When I come home to our apartment in the evenings, I want to find a serious adult there. His idea of playing dress-up turns me off. All I want is a nice meal and a hot shower."

"That about describes our sex life. Except, it is more like a quick meal and a cold shower," sulked Gregg.

Differences in sexual taste present a problem shared by many couples. A man's sexual taste is often extremely different from that of a woman. He may want her to wear thigh-high boots and a leather bra. His idea of a turn-on might be to discover she is wearing no underwear at all under her cocktail dress on a Saturday evening. A woman's idea of attracting her mate's sexual attention may be to spend hours in a beauty salon having her hair and nails done or spend a week's salary on a new black dress and fabulous eye shadow. Paradoxically, although this may be a woman's idea of arousing a man, often, when her mate tries to touch her, she pushes him away exclaiming that he will mess her hair and makeup. In Janice and Gregg's situation, Gregg wishes Janice would go to more trouble to make herself sexually attractive for him. He wants to interject a little sexual fantasy into their lives.

All people have sexual fantasies. Not all people act on them. Sexual fantasy can often satisfy mates on various levels. It can be titillating and illuminating play. Fantasy enables partners to behave sexually in a less inhibited way. In sexual play or sexual storytelling, a couple's spontaneity can be revived. Sexual fantasy can be a release as well as an infinite source for sexual variety with a loved and trusted partner.

Some mates do feel threatened when a partner first presents the idea of sexual fantasy into lovemaking. A mate may feel it is unnatural or unhealthy. A mate may wonder if a partner is dissatisfied with making love in familiar ways. A woman may have been taught by her mother and society that "Nice girls just don't do those things." Those words somehow get translated into the bedroom years after a woman has become an adult. Although it may be difficult for her at first, a woman can learn to overcome these ideas. It is often necessary for her to remember that lessons learned in childhood that were appropriate to protect her as a girl are no longer needed with a loving mate now that she is a woman. It is equally important to remember that no one should be forced to engage in sexual fantasy. If Janice agrees to try to experiment with her loving partner, they might find new and exciting ways to please each other that they are both comfortable with.

It is not helpful for Janice to ask Gregg how he could have imagined she would enjoy this outfit. When a woman says she can't believe a man would spend money on anything so stupid, she is belittling his taste and ridiculing his ideas. Janice could choose to remember that Gregg views her as an exotic female and bite her tongue. She could tell Gregg she is flattered that he sees her as a sexual being. She could express her appreciation and tell him that she understands that he purchased the harem outfit out of feelings of love for her.

Janice might explain to Gregg that she feels uncomfortable wearing such an outfit, *at this time*. She could suggest they go shopping together to choose something that is a little more comfortable for her and still exciting to him. When partners choose something together for sexual fantasy, including the fantasy itself, they are saying they care enough to try. In time, Janice may feel very comfortable wearing the harem outfit or the motorcycle chaps or whatever they find mutually sexually exciting. Couples need to remember that being willing to make an effort to fulfill a partner's exotic fantasy will go a long way toward helping couples become more sexually creative.

Whether a couple chooses to engage in sexual fantasy or experiment in tying each others arms and legs with silk scarves to the bed posts, the most important thing to remember is that in order to have a successful sexual relationship couples need to communicate feelings to each other. Giving 200 percent to a relationship is the most effective way of communicating how much a partner cares. When lovers speak to each other, they really need to look into each other's eyes. A good lover is sensitive and caring and expresses that love and care in every way a partner can conceive.

Being in love makes partners feel completely connected to each other and to the rest of the world. When mates love, all feelings of separateness seem to disappear. Love is universally felt in this way. It is not a gift from someone else. Love is a gift a partner gives to him- or herself. Love is a realization that requires constant attention.

Although lovers experience hurt, anger, and sometimes even fear with each other, to be successful lovers, it is imperative to be totally committed to creating a loving and harmonious atmosphere, no matter what the obstacles. It takes courage to see love in a partner, even when that partner is unable to believe it is there.

Love is probably the greatest adventure in all of life. Successful lovers prepare for the adventure. Love requires constant training. It also requires being intimately knowledgeable about one's self. When a partner is open to discovery, learns to be compatible, and is willing to adjust and grow, the winning combination of sex and love are certain to be attained.

Conclusion

Throughout this book, there are numerous examples of sexual problems experienced by couples involved in intimate relationships. Do any of these situations sound familiar? Unfortunately, sexual problems cannot be simply categorized. Because there are as many different types of sexual problems as there are people, identifying a problem is often half the battle. Sometimes a trained professional can be very helpful.

Remember, the strongest attribute in any sexual relationship is communication. Being honest with a partner, of course, does not mean being brutal. Being equal does not necessarily mean mates are equal at the same time. Issues of concern for one partner may not be valid for another. It is important to set goals in a relationship that will allow a sense of purpose and fulfillment for both mates. Partners need to be assured they are trustworthy and cherished. Couples *can learn* to communicate in a loving, caring way. When partners work together to achieve shared goals, to listen to, enjoy, and understand each other's hopes and dreams, sexual fulfillment most certainly will be the reward.

Although it is true that no long-term relationship is without feelings of anger and resentment, hurt and bewilderment, it is possible to develop true understanding, support, and a sense of humor. Don't forget to enjoy the journey and recharge the batteries in your relationship often. When you and your partner are able to leave yourselves open for discovery, take the long and winding roads instead of the freeways, eternal love will most certainly be the destination. Rediscovering the delights, the exhilaration, and the suspense of the backseat can be the adventure of a lifetime!

Bibliography

Barbach, Lonnie Garfield. *For Yourself: The Fulfillment of Female Sexuality.* New York: Doubleday, 1976.

Barbach, Lonnie, Ph.D. *For Each Other: Sharing Sexual Intimacy.* New York: Doubleday, 1982.

Beaver, Daniel, M.S., M.F.C.C. *More Than Just Sex.* Lower Lake, California: Asian Publishing, 1992.

Bloomfield, Harold, M.D. *Lifemates.* New York: New American Library, 1992.

Branden, Nathaniel. *The Psychology of Romantic Love.* New York: Bantam, 1981.

Cohen, Sherry Suib. *The Secrets of a Very Good Marriage.* New York: Carol Southern, 1993.

Covey, Stephen R. *The 7 Habits of Highly Effective People.* New York: Simon and Schuster, 1989.

DeAngelis, Barbara, Ph.D. *Are You the One for Me?* New York: Dell Publishing, 1992.

DeAngelis, Barbara, Ph.D. *Secrets About Men Every Woman Should Know.* New York: Dell Publishing, 1990.

Dolesh, Daniel J. and Sherelynn Lehman. *Love Me, Love Me Not: How to Survive Infidelity.* New York: McGraw-Hill Book Co., 1985.

Farrell, Warren. *Why Men Are the Way They Are.* New York: McGraw-Hill, 1986.

Fisher, Helen, Ph.D. *Anatomy of Love*. New York: Ballantine Books, 1992.

Friday, Nancy. *Women on Top*. New York: Pocket Books, 1991.

Godek, Gregory J. P. *1001 Ways To Be Romantic*. Boston: Casablanca Press, 1993.

Gray, John, Ph.D. *Men Are From Mars, Women Are From Venus*. New York: Harper Collins, 1992.

Hendricks, Gay and Katherine Hendricks. *Conscious Loving: The Journey to Commitment*. New York: Bantam, 1990.

Hendrix, Harville, Ph.D. *Getting the Love You Want: A Guide for Couples*. New York: Harper and Row, 1988.

Hite, Shere. *The Hite Report*. New York: MacMillan Publishing, 1976.

Hutton, Julia. *Good Sex*. Pittsburgh: Cleis Press, 1992.

Janus, Samuel, S. Ph.D. and Cynthia L. Janus, M.D. *The Janus Report on Sexual Behavior*. New York: John Wiley and Sons, 1993.

Johnson, Robert A. *We: Understanding the Psychology of Romantic Love*. San Francisco: Harper and Row, 1983.

Kaplan, Helen Singer, M.D., Ph.D. *The Illustrated Manual of Sex Therapy*, 2nd ed. New York: Brunner/Mazel, 1987.

Klein, Marty. *Ask Me Anything*. New York: Simon and Schuster, 1992.

Lerner, Harriet Goldhor, Ph.D. *The Dance of Intimacy*. New York: Harper and Row, 1989.

Kreidman, Ellen. *Light His Fire*. New York: Dell Publishing, 1989.

Masters, William H., Virginia Johnson, and Robert C. Koladny. *Masters and Johnson on Sex and Human Behavior*. Boston: Little, Brown and Co., 1988.

Moyers, Bill. *Healing the Mind*. New York: Doubleday, 1993.

Pearsall, Paul, Ph.D. *Super Marital Sex*. New York: Ballantine Books, 1987.

Peck, M. Scott. *The Road Less Traveled*. New York: Simon and Schuster, 1980.

Reinisch, June M., Ph.D. with Ruth Beasley, M.L.S. *The Kinsey Institute New Report on Sex.* New York: St. Martin's Press, 1990.

Rhodes, Carol L., Ph.D. and Norman S. Goldner, Ph.D. *Why Women and Men Don't Get Along!* Troy, Michigan: Somerset, 1993.

Rubin, Lillian B. *Intimate Strangers: Men and Women Together.* New York: Harper and Row, 1983.

Scarf, Maggie. *Intimate Partners: Patterns of Love in Marriage.* New York: Random House, 1987.

Schloff, Laurie and Marcia Yudkin. *He & She Talk: How To Communicate with the Opposite Sex.* New York: Penguin Books, 1993.

Slung, Michele. *Slow Hand: Women Writing Erotica.* New York: Harper Collins, 1992.

Stuart, Richard B. *Helping Couples Change.* New York: The Guilford Press, 1980.

Tanenbaum, Joe. *Male and Female Realities: Understanding the Opposite Sex.* Sugar Land, Texas: Candle Publishing, 1989.

Tannen, Deborah, Ph.D. *You Just Don't Understand.* New York: William Morrow and Company, 1990.

Tessubam, Tina and Riley K. Smith. *How to Be a Couple and Still Be Free.* New York: Putnam, 1993.

Viorst, Judith. *Necessary Losses.* New York: Simon and Schuster, 1987.

Zilbergeld, Bernie, Ph.D. *The New Male Sexuality.* New York: Bantam Books, 1992.

Index

About the Authors

Sherry Lehman is a certified Sex Therapist and a licensed Marriage and Family Therapist, operating in private practice in Cleveland, Ohio. She has hosted several radio talk shows, including "Sexline" and "The Sherry Lehman Show" and appears regularly on local and national television talk shows. She is the co-author of *Love Me, Love Me Not: How to Survive Infidelity*.

Micki Brook is a freelance writer who wrote for *Psychology Today* magazine for almost ten years. Micki hosts a daily radio talk show in Cleveland called "Fifty Something," dedicated to making the next fifty years of life better than the first.